IMAGES
of America

PARMA

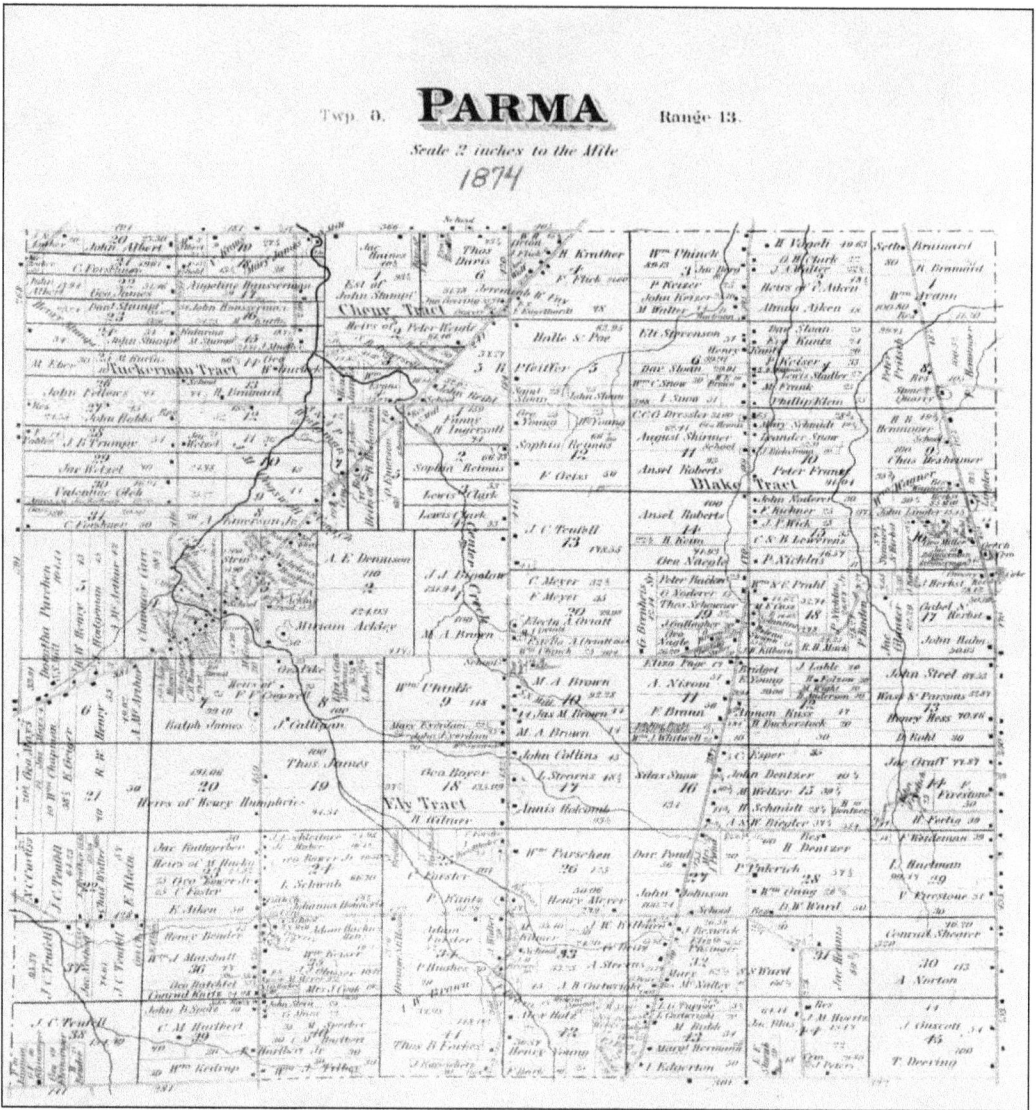

PARMA MAP, 1874. This is a map of Parma from 1874 as it was once laid out. It was said that Thomas Jefferson set up cities in such a way that the city hall would always be in the exact center of town. (Courtesy of Cuyahoga County Public Library Parma-South Branch.)

ON THE COVER: Residents of Parma celebrate Parma Day in 1936. Parma Day was an annual celebration in which the community would gather together for a day of fun and games. That year's attraction was a freckle contest, and the person with the most freckles won a prize. Parma Day had a high attendance in 1936 with over 15,000 people. (Courtesy of Cleveland Press Collection.)

IMAGES
of America

PARMA

Diana J. Eid

ARCADIA
PUBLISHING

Published by Arcadia Publishing
Charleston, South Carolina

Library of Congress Control Number: 2009933846

For all general information contact Arcadia Publishing at:
Telephone 843-853-2070
Fax 843-853-0044
E-mail sales@arcadiapublishing.com
For customer service and orders:
Toll-Free 1-888-313-2665

Visit us on the Internet at www.arcadiapublishing.com

CONTENTS

ACKNOWLEDGMENTS

There are so many people that helped me with this book. First of all, I'd like to thank Lynn Duchez Bycko at the Cleveland State University Special Collections Library for helping me get started and pulling out the many Parma photographs over and over again.

Mayor James W. Day spent quite a bit of time with me, and his impeccable memory in remembering dates and places was very beneficial. Thank you to Jim Griffith at the Parma Heights Historical Society for allowing me to look through the archives, which filled in some much-needed information. Myrtis Litman found some local connections and made some important phone calls. I am grateful to Ruth Fay for the use of her family pictures and for inviting me into her home to talk about her ancestors. Beth Foster spent countless hours with me driving the streets of Parma and listened to me talk endlessly about my favorite city.

I would like to thank the West Creek Preservation Committee for providing me with valuable information on preserving the city's historic landmarks.

Thank you to Tom Mastroianni and Ken Ramser, who were also a huge help in getting me started by connecting me with certain people to talk to. The City of Parma employees are also due a big thank you, as they had a lot of knowledge about the past and present. I'd also like to thank the Parma Area Historical Society for letting me look through their collections and also for accepting me as their newest volunteer. My father, Richard Eid, let me use his store to write this book while I was supposed to be working. Thanks, Dad.

My editor at Arcadia Publishing, Melissa Basilone, was great and is definitely owed a special thank you for helping me on my first book.

Finally I'd like to thank my mother, Susan Eid, who helped and motivated me every step of the way. Without her amazing scanning and phone skills, as well as her daily motivation, I would have had a very hard time finishing this book. You are the best, Mom. Thank you for everything.

INTRODUCTION

What was Parma before it became the big city it is today? To get an idea, the area known in the Western Reserve as Township 6, Range 13 was once called Greenbrier after the many thorny bushes that filled the area. Imagine traveling by foot or wagon hundreds of miles to arrive at a destination only to have to hack a clearing out of the woods. That is just what the first settlers did when they arrived in the area in 1816. In doing so, they made that clearing their home and soon set out to build up the land. The first settler was a merchant and soon after arriving saw an opportunity for business. In 1819, this merchant and his family built a home and turned it into an inn and tavern. Business soon began to thrive as more settlers landed in the area. People in Cleveland were referring to the area as Briar Hill. Somewhere along the line, a medical doctor in Cleveland named Dr. David Long visited the Duchy of Parma, Italy, and was very impressed with the area. He came back into town and persuaded the people of Greenbrier that they should have a better name. He suggested the name of Parma to them, which they accepted.

In 1826, the township of Parma was formed when settlers separated themselves from Brooklyn Township. It was also in this year that the first and second school districts were formed. Parma was steadily on its way. Around this time, the town was also divided into road districts, and many roads had simple names. For instance, Ridge Road was once called Center Road, mainly because it ran through the center of town.

By 1840, there were 963 people living in Parma. While the land was quickly becoming occupied with new arrivals, there was still a problem with the number of bears, wolves, and rattlesnakes that were destroying farm animals and crops. In 1842, a hunting party was organized and lasted several days in an attempt to rid the area of these animals that were wreaking havoc. From 1850 to 1910, Parma's population growth slowed down, as there was very little land available for purchase, having been used mostly for farming. Early records show that a few businesses were already in the community. In 1876, there were blacksmith shops and repair shops in the area, while grocery stores were many miles apart from each other.

Around this time, Parma and its surrounding towns were expanding as bridges and plank roads were now being built. In 1912, a portion of Parma broke off and became known as Parma Heights. Some say it had to do with the Temperance Movement, which was a social movement against the use of alcohol. Since Parma had an abundance of taverns and inns, many believed the people of Parma Heights wanted to form their own community that would give them the right to make their own laws and government. The U.S. census of 1920 listed Parma Heights's population at 310, while Parma had 2,345 people.

After World War I, many developers started looking at land in the area. They wanted to build, and soon after many homes appeared in Parma. Howard A. Stahl was Parma's first major land developer and was responsible for much of the layout of Parma's streets today. The dinkey streetcar soon became a regular fixture for transportation in the area. In 1924, the people voted and Parma was incorporated as a village. The first mayor of the village of Parma was John F. Goldenbogen.

During this time, a new town hall was built. The previous one had been in an old schoolhouse at Ridge Road and Bean Road (now Ridgewood Drive). The city continued to thrive. In 1927, Parma was considered Cleveland's fastest-growing suburb. With a population of 2,345 in 1920, by 1930 it was booming with over 13,000 people. More schools were being constructed as well as businesses and homes.

Parma became a city in 1931. However, it wasn't as joyous an occasion as it should have been. The 1930s saw the Depression, which had an effect everywhere, including Parma. Wages of employees were cut in order to keep the city afloat, and many people were unemployed at the time. There was talk of the city and school district annexing to Cleveland, but the people took a vote and decided against it. By the beginning of the 1940s, Parma was beginning to emerge again with more growth around the city.

After World War II ended, many soldiers came home and needed a place to raise their families. Many of them moved to Parma. Abandoned streets were rebuilt, and new homes sprouted up everywhere. The 1940s and 1950s saw much growth to the industrial side of the city. The General Motors Chevrolet Plant was being constructed in 1947, and the Union Carbide Research Center was established as well. More schools were being built to keep up with the growing area. In 1950, the population was over 28,000, but by 1960 it had tripled to more than 82,000 people. The 1960s saw many shopping plazas pop up in the area as well as Parmatown Mall. Parma Community General Hospital also opened its doors during this time. Even a new city hall was built to keep up with the city's rapid expansion. Parma was known at this time as the fastest-growing city not only in Ohio, but also in the United States.

Parma is a unique city and has had its share of visitors. From the president stopping by to make a speech, to local comedians doing spoofs on Parma, each and every event has made this city into what it is today. It is interesting to note that no one person can be credited with shaping the city. The first settlers might have had a vision of what they wanted Parma to be, and along the way every citizen of the city, even now, has united to keep Parma strong. The city is still growing, but one thing remains the same, and that is the loyalty each resident has to preserving the history of the city as well as expanding on it for the future generations.

Welcome to Parma, Ohio. I hope you enjoy your stay.

One

IN THE BEGINNING

In 1816, a man named Benajah Fay, his wife, Ruth, and their 10 children arrived on a piece of land identified by the Western Reserve as Township 6, Range 13. They decided to make this area their home. Benajah and Ruth had come from Lewis County, New York, and they most likely arrived in this area for the land and better opportunities. The family soon set out to clear a patch of land in which to live on. They settled on what is now Theota Avenue at the intersection of Pearl and Ridge Roads.

About a year later, another family arrived, and soon thereafter Parma had a small group of settlers who had decided to stay in this area. Benajah and Ruth had the first child born in Parma, in 1820, and named her Mabel. The first death in Parma was that of Isaac Emerson, in 1823, and the first marriage in Parma took place between Lois Small of Parma and Ephraim Fowles of Middleburg Heights.

By 1820, the inn and tavern that Benajah worked to build was becoming a busy place, as it was the "No. 2 stop" on the Cleveland-Columbus stagecoach line. Blacksmith and repair shops as well as schools and churches were erected in the area, as the residents decided that they wanted to stay and build on this land that they had chosen to settle on. By 1850, Parma had around 1,500 people living in the area, which was a big change from 1816 when there were only 12.

As more settlers arrived, they brought unique skills. This chapter shows early images of Parma citizens as far back as the late 1800s. While the farms and businesses are no longer there, these photographs serve as reminders of how the early residents lived and what they did to help Parma grow.

PARMA'S FIRST BUSINESS ESTABLISHMENT. Benajah Fay's homestead was first built in 1819. It had two sections, one for the family and one for the inn that was named B. Fay's Inn. It quickly became a busy place, being the No. 2 stop on the stagecoach line that traveled from Cleveland to Columbus. As business grew, Fay replaced the house in 1832 with one built out of sun-dried brick. This house was located on the east side of Pearl Road at Theota Avenue. (Courtesy of Ruth Fay.)

BENAJAH FAY HOMESTEAD. This is a view of the south side of the house on Pearl and Ridge Roads, built in 1832 and razed in 1912. The house had loft sleeping areas for travelers as well as accommodations for their horses. Eventually sawmills were added, which put up sawed lumber for sale. This is the first brick house in Parma Township. (Courtesy of Ruth Fay.)

LETTER TO BENAJAH FAY. This letter, dated around 1820 and written to "Dear Brother," was sent to Fay. The envelope was only addressed as "Benajah Fay / State of Ohio / The town of Cleveland." Surprisingly, the letter was received. Back around those times, it usually took a week or more to receive mail because it was delivered by horse. This letter is written to Fay by his sister Mary McCallister. She is writing to tell him that they had just left York State (New York) and came down the Ohio River and then up the Mississippi to the village of Milton. The letter also mentions an "angry fever," which has caused the sickness and deaths of many people. The fever that the writer is referring to was most likely yellow fever, which infected and killed many people during that time. (Courtesy of Ruth Fay.)

11

JEREMIAH AND MARYANN BRADLEY FAY. Pictured here around the late 1800s are the Fays on the porch of their homestead. Jeremiah Wilcox Fay was born in 1822 and was the youngest son of Benajah Fay. The furniture they are seated on was given to them in 1854 as a wedding gift. The furniture has been restored and is still in use today by their descendants. (Courtesy of Ruth Fay.)

ON THE HOMESTEAD. This picture, taken in the late 1800s, shows Jeremiah and his wife, Maryann Bradley Fay, at the well on their homestead. Before water wells, people often had to carry water by foot from a stream or pond that was sometimes located miles away. Some families were able to use a horse and wagon to carry water back to their homestead. (Courtesy of Ruth Fay.)

CLARENCE STEVENS. This photograph, taken in the late 1930s, shows Clarence Stevens harvesting crops in a field located between Lawndale and Woodview Avenues. There was an apple orchard in the background that is said to have been planted by Johnny Appleseed. (Courtesy of Ruth Fay.)

HARVESTING CROPS. Taken sometime in the late 1800s to early 1900s, pictured here in a field are, from left to right, unidentified, Maryann Bradley Fay, and Ruth Stevens Fay. Back then, horses were used to plow fields and spread grain in order to make crops grow. Today modern equipment makes the process go more quickly. (Courtesy of Ruth Fay.)

COURT SUMMONS. This document from 1835 is a court summons issued by Justice of the Peace Oliver Emerson. His father, Asa Emerson, was one of the early settlers in Parma. This document called at least 10 people to appear in court on May 2, 1835. These witnesses were subjected to a $50 fine if they failed to appear. (Courtesy of Parma Heights Historical Society.)

GIBBS HOUSE, 1969. The small house in the background of this photograph was built by Lyman Stearns around 1855. Earl Gibbs bought the farm around 1920 and built the white house shown. He raised beef and cattle on the farm through the 1970s. In 1980, the City of Parma bought the property from the Gibbs family and licensed it to the Parma Area Historical Society, which now operates the farm. In 1981, the farm was placed on the National Register of Historic Places. (Courtesy of Cleveland Press Collection.)

TORNADO GOES THROUGH PARMA. This picture was taken around 1911, right after a tornado hit in the area. This barn, located at the southwest corner of Ridge and Pearl Roads, was one of the structures that became twisted. Notice how the people are trying to salvage the barn by supporting it with wooden beams. (Courtesy of Ruth Fay.)

SOUTHEAST CORNER OF PEARL AND BROOKPARK ROADS. This photograph was taken around 1911 and is possibly the same disaster as above. This tornado demolished resident Otto Thompson's house, killing his wife, Lottie. The tornado completely destroyed some houses while leaving others unharmed. Many crops could not be salvaged. (Courtesy of Ruth Fay.)

CLARENCE FAY, EARLY 1900S. Clarence Fay was born in 1873 at the Fay homestead. His father was Jeremiah Wilcox Fay, who was believed to be the first white male born in Parma in 1822. Clarence married Ruth R. Stevens and had five children. He and his family would often shop at the People's Grocery Store, which was at Pearl and Broadview Roads. Their grocery bill for the week was usually $2 or $3. (Courtesy of Ruth Fay.)

THE STEVENS FAMILY. This photograph, taken around the 1890s, shows the Stevens family wearing Victorian-style hats, which were popular at the time. From left to right are Ruth R. Fay (wife of Clarence Fay), Irma Bordine, Albert Stevens, and Bertha M. Hodgman. (Courtesy of Ruth Fay.)

WOODCUTTERS. This photograph shows Albert Stevens (left) and his father, Clarence Stevens, splitting wood for their wood-fired stoves, which were used for cooking as well as heat. Woodcutting and farming were the main industries in Parma during this time. (Courtesy of Ruth Fay.)

ST. PAULUS CHURCH, LATE 1800s. This image was taken sometime around 1890 and shows the founding members of the church now known as St. Paul United Church of Christ located at York and Pleasant Valley Roads. The people are standing in front of the first church, which was built in 1858. (Courtesy of St. Paul United Church of Christ.)

HENNINGER HOUSE. The Henninger House is located at 5757 Broadview Road near Snow and Rockside Roads. It was built in 1849 by Philip and Sophia Henninger and is currently the oldest home in Parma. It is in the style of vernacular Greek Revival. The house has survived four generations of Henningers and now remains unoccupied. There is a barn near the back that was built before the house was constructed. That barn is considered the oldest structure in Parma. Threatened to be torn down for commercial sale and development, the Henninger House was saved by a grassroots effort and today continues to be one of the memorable landmarks in Parma. The photograph above was taken in the mid-1800s, while the image below is a current view. (Above, courtesy of Parma Area Historical Society; below, Westcreek Preservation Committee.)

PHILIP HENNINGER. Philip Henninger was born on October 20, 1813, in Germany. He and his wife, Sophia Orth Henninger, came to the United States in 1830 and settled in Parma Township. Philip was a tinsmith and provided services from his barn. (Courtesy of West Creek Preservation Committee.)

SOPHIA HENNINGER, c. 1900. Sophia was born on May 9, 1823, in Germany. When Sophia turned 18, she married Philip. They built a log cabin on their property and had their first child, Helen, in 1842. Philip and Sophia are buried at St. Peter's Church Cemetery on Broadview Road. (Courtesy of West Creek Preservation Committee.)

HENNINGER FAMILY. The Henninger House had a summer kitchen, which was located in the back of the home and had ventilation all throughout in order to make cooking easier and cooler during the hotter months. The Henningers had 10 children, the first being born in 1842 and the last in 1858. Their names were Helen, John, Henry, Louisa, Louis, Emma, Laura, Julia, Maria, and Mary. (Courtesy of West Creek Preservation Committee.)

HENNINGER HOMESTEAD. Sitting on the porch enjoying the afternoon are, from left to right, Henninger, Uhinck, and Bayer. Neighbors often lived far away from each other, so getting together was a special event. A woman shown in the background is wearing an apron to cook a big meal for the day. (Courtesy of West Creek Preservation Committee.)

HENNINGER HOUSE BACK PORCH. This picture, taken on the back porch, is dated around 1900 and shows Sophia Henninger on the far right. The house was built on a hill facing north and sits on one of the highest points in Cuyahoga County. (Courtesy of West Creek Preservation Committee.)

CARRIAGE RIDE. This photograph, taken around 1913, is at the site of the Jacob Fleck farm in Parma. The location was at the confluence of Wooster Pike Road (now Pearl Road), Brookpark Road, and Center Road (now Ridge Road). The ground was very high and all farmland. Pictured here are, from left to right, Margaret Emerson, Mildred Emerson Wood, Kenneth Emerson, and Ernest Emerson holding the reins. (Courtesy of Parma Heights Historical Society.)

ACKLEY FAMILY. Shown here is Mr. Ackley with his daughter Helen. Ackley Street was named after this man, who owned property in the area. He also owned land at Stearns Homestead and sold one-third of this property to the Stearns family, where they built the barn and the small house. (Courtesy of Parma Heights Historical Society.)

COGSWELL FAMILY. Dewitt Cogswell (far left) was born on March 22, 1891. In 1917, he married Marguerite Rose from Sharon, Pennsylvania. He had a farm located on York Road. Shown here in the early 1900s is the Cogswell family on their farm. Dewitt attended District No. 9 School, which was located where the Parma Heights City Hall now stands. (Courtesy of the Parma Area Historical Society.)

22

THE THRESHER GANG. Threshing, also known as thrashing, is part of the harvesting process used to separate grain from stalks and husks. Shown above is the threshing gang in the early 1900s during their mid-afternoon lunchtime. Women would prepare big meals for the men working the fields. This happened twice a year, once during threshing time and the other during silo filling. Shown below around the same time period is an early threshing machine being pulled by a coal-burning engine. A caption placed on this picture stated that coal was $2.50 to $3.00 per ton but that air pollution was free. (Both courtesy of the Kaiser family.)

HAYSTACK, EARLY 1900s. After threshing, the men would rake off the loose straw and then add weight to the top of the pile. This prevented the wind from blowing the straw stack down the road or over to the next-door neighbor's field, thereby losing hours of hard work. (Courtesy of the Kaiser family.)

THE ARM BREAKER. Shown here in 1916 is George Kaiser with a Model T Ford that was purchased for $440. The Model T was often referred to as a "Tin Lizzie." Lizzie was the name given at the time for a reliable servant. It also earned the nickname "The Arm Breaker" because it had to be hand-cranked in order to get it running. At the time, gasoline was 15¢ a gallon. (Courtesy of the Kaiser family.)

APPLE BUTTER. Katherine Kaiser is shown here stirring one of many kettles of apple butter that were made twice a year. Apples were usually picked by the children on Friday in order to start the apple butter process on Saturday. The whole family peeled, cored, then quartered the apples in order to take them to the cider mill to have them ground and pressed. This orchard was located just south of the entrance to Crile Hospital, which is now Cuyahoga Community College. (Courtesy of the Kaiser family.)

DOGSLEDDER, C. 1914. Mike Doss is posing with his sled and dog. His father made a harness for the dog, and they trained the dog with a piece of sausage that dangled about 6 inches in front of it. The dog would repeatedly try to catch the sausage and soon became trained to pull the sled. (Courtesy of the Kaiser family.)

OUT IN THE FIELD. Taken around 1913, George Kaiser is on his farm reaping oats in a horse-drawn wagon. Later on, horses were replaced by tractors in the field. This farm was located in the York and Moore Roads area. (Courtesy of the Kaiser family.)

SATURDAY AFTERNOON RIDE. Grandpa Bauer is shown here around 1915. The buggy in this photograph had rubber tires, which had been put on just after the end of steel tires. The cost of this buggy was $110, which included the horse blanket. (Courtesy of the Kaiser family.)

SUNDAY SCHOOL. Shown here in 1916 is a Sunday school class. These boys are on Bean Road (now Ridgewood Drive) walking from the State Road dinkey to Ridge Road. They were most likely heading to the Uhinck family homestead, a family that came to Parma in 1845 from Mannheim, Germany, and settled at what is now the intersection of Ridge Road and Day Drive. (Courtesy of Parma Area Historical Society.)

ASA EMERSON HOUSE. This photograph, taken around 1834, is of the homestead of Asa Emerson. Emerson was born on October 30, 1812, in Bowdoin, Maine. He came to Parma in 1821 with his parents and remained here until his death in 1898. The address of this house is 6103 Pearl Road, and it still stands today. (Courtesy of Parma Heights Historical Society.)

AMOS DENISON HOME. This home, located at 6037 Pearl Road, was occupied by Amos Denison. It was also a stop on the Underground Railroad. Denison hid slaves in his barn and would drive them to the next stop in his wagon, which was specially designed to hide people. (Courtesy of Parma Heights Historical Society.)

HOUSE ON PEARL ROAD. This home at 6363 Pearl Road in Parma Heights was said to have been built in the 1800s. It was originally a tavern on the Cleveland-Columbus stagecoach line and was located near Pearl Road and Kingsdale Boulevard. It was often referred to as "The Old Stone Tavern." This house was believed to be owned by Conrad Countryman, who in 1817 was the second settler to arrive in Parma. (Courtesy of Cleveland Press Collection.)

MABEL FOOTE. Mabel Foote, 24 years old, taught freshmen and sophomore students in a schoolhouse located on Ridge Road. She and 38-year-old Louise Wolf, who taught juniors and seniors, were killed in a February 1921 tragedy. Wolf and Foote had been on their way to ride the dinkey when they were brutally attacked in a crime that was never solved. (Courtesy of Cleveland Public Library Photograph Collection.)

PARMA HIGH SCHOOL, 1921. This is the school that Foote taught at. It was located at Ridge and Bean Roads (Ridgewood Drive). Wolf taught her classes in a school that was located directly across the street from this one. In 1932, a small park was dedicated to the memory of the two teachers. The memorial is located at the south end of the Brookside Bridge on Pearl Road at the entrance to Brookside Park. (Courtesy of Cleveland Press Collection.)

29

PARMA CONSTABLE, 1921. After the horrible murders of the two teachers, the township was enraged. Shortly afterwards, a constabulary was formed in order to keep peace in the area. This image shows Conrad Riedthaler, one of the men appointed to the constabulary. (Courtesy of Cleveland Public Library Photograph Collection.)

BEAN ROAD. This image from 1921 shows Bean Road, which is now Ridgewood Drive. Children and teachers often walked this road to State Road, where they would catch the dinkey streetcar to and from school. The area in this photograph is now where city hall resides. (Courtesy of Parma Area Historical Society.)

Two

SCHOOLS AND CHURCHES

Early records show that the first classes were held in the home of resident Samuel Freeman. Freeman was not only the first schoolteacher, but he also served as the first justice of the peace and first postmaster of the township. With Parma's population growth, trustees met on May 13, 1826, to form the first school district in Parma Township. The first schoolhouse was located on what is now the Parma Heights Cemetery on Pearl Road. It was used for schooling, meetings, elections, and religious services until 1841. A plaque mounted on a boulder in the cemetery marks the location of where this school used to be. The township first started with two school districts and later split into nine. As time went on, many schools were built in the area to accommodate the growing number of children attending classes.

The Parma School District is the 2nd largest in Cuyahoga County and the 11th largest in Ohio. Made up of Parma, Parma Heights, and Seven Hills, the district currently has 20 schools. This includes three high schools, three middle schools, 13 elementary schools and one special-needs preschool. This chapter highlights some of the schools in the area.

Parma is also known for its many places of worship and has often been referred to as "A City of Churches." The first religious service was held in 1822 by Rev. Henry Hudson at the home of early settler Asa Emerson. The first church in Parma was the Free Will Baptist Church, which started around 1830 and was located in the southeast corner of the township. Featured here are some of the older churches that were started in Parma in the late 1800s to the 1930s.

What began as a small gathering of worshipers in 1822 has now led to Parma becoming a home to over 50 churches, including a Byzantine cathedral and a Ukrainian Catholic church, as well as one of the nation's largest Islamic mosques.

EARLY SCHOOL PHOTOGRAPH. The first schoolhouse was built out of logs and sat on top of a hill in the Parma Heights Cemetery on Pearl Road. As the population grew, more schools were needed, and soon nine one-room buildings were added around town. This photograph was taken at a school in Parma in the early 1900s. (Courtesy of the Kaiser family.)

CLASS OF 1896. Pictured here are, from left to right, (first row) Fred Gerspacher, Fred Wengatz, Frank Gerspacher, Fred Uhinck, Frank Brown, Henry Riedthaler, Earl Pickard, and Adolph Wengatz; (second row) Elnor Brown, Harry Gerspacher, Eda Uhinck, Elva Geiss, Jennie Krist, Elsa Uhinck, Jake Krist, Gertrude Krist, and Emma Uhinck; (third row, those standing) Robert Uhinck, Walter Shuh, Elsie Brown, Marion Jones, Dora Meyer, Miss Husband, Mame Riedthaler, Kate Riedthaler, Mable Wengatz, Julius Oberdoerster, and Lottie Uhinck. (Courtesy of Parma Heights Historical Society.)

STUDENTS. Shown here is teacher Frank Blair with his students. Blair was paid $30 per month at the time to teach. Teachers were offered an extra $3 if they cleaned the schoolroom as well as kept the school fires burning. (Courtesy of the Kaiser family.)

EARLY 1900S CLASS. Seen here are, from left to right, (first row) Henry Koch, Mike Schneider, Harold Goodin, Frank Kortz, Louis Schwab, Marcus Rohrbach, and Charlie Goodin; (second row) Annie Nothoff, Alma Spatz, Clara Doss, Gertrude Reuss, Frances and Rosa Thiele, Frieda Hortz, George Bauer, and Joe Nothoff; (third row) Alfred Kortz, Alma and Lizzie Nothoff, Alma Schneider, Alvie Kaiser, Mary Doss, Arnold Bauer, Fred Koch, Arthur Schmitendorf, and Carl Kaiser; (fourth row) Marie Reuss, Dora Koch, Theresa Rohrbach, Will Schwab, Frank Blair, Margaret Nothoff, Clara Hagen, Hulda Spatz, and Carl Hagen. (Courtesy of the Kaiser family.)

ELEMENTARY SCHOOL, 1912. Pictured here is the District No. 1 Elementary School at Pearl and Snow Roads. Parma had nine individually run school districts that were eventually consolidated. In this image is teacher Florence Hagan with her students. Two of the boys in this photograph are Eugene Fay and Dudley Fay, both descendants of Benajah Fay. (Courtesy of Ruth Fay.)

CLASS PHOTOGRAPH. This picture, taken during the 1933–1934 school year, shows the third-grade class of Pearl Road School. The teacher pictured is Opal McClarren, who later married Dudley Fay. During this time, schools did not hire married women. Some members of this class still get together once a month and talk about old times. (Courtesy of Ruth Fay.)

BASEBALL GAME, EARLY 1900S. Playing baseball in the backyard are the children from District No. 3 Pleasant Valley Road School located near Pleasant Valley and York Roads. The batter is Carl Kaiser. Children often played games during recess such as Pump Pump Pull Away, Crack the Whip, Fox and Geese, and Two Old Cat baseball. (Courtesy of the Kaiser family.)

PARMA SCHOOL BUS. Shown here is an early school bus around 1928. Many children did not attend school during the months of May through November because there was a lot of work to be done on the farm during those times. (Courtesy of Parma Area Historical Society.)

Parma Senior Commencement

AT

PARMA HIGH SCHOOL

JUNE 1, 1922   -   8:00 P. M.

Program

Invocation . . . . . Rev. J. S. Eaton
Song   [Little Boy Blue]   by the 8th grade of the Ridge Road School
Salutatory . . . . . Caroline Larsen
Vocal Solo . . . . . Mrs. Howard Ingham
Class Address   "What is Winning?" . . Sen. J. F. Burke
Duet "Watchman, What of the Night?"   { Mr. John Eaton
                                       { Mr. Howard Ingham
Valedictory . . . . . Hilda Haas
Vocal Solo . . . . . Mr. John Eaton
Presentation of Diplomas and School Charter
                      by Supt. of Schools A. G. Yawberg
Benediction . . . . . Rev. Eaton

CLASS ROLL

Hilda Haas   Caroline Larsen
   Ella Hoffman   Laura Ward
      Paul Crouch   Eugene Fay

Class Motto   - - -   *Wish less, do more*

Class Flower   -   *American Beauty Rose*

Class Colors   - - -   *Green and Gold*

PARMA SENIOR COMMENCEMENT PROGRAM, JUNE 1922. These students were the first graduating class in Parma. Before then, Parma never had a high school class graduate. Parma High School was located at Ridge Road and Day Drive near Byers Field. (Courtesy of Ruth Fay.)

STUDENT REPORT CARD. This is the report card for Dudley Fay in 1917. He was in fifth grade at the time at District No. 1 School at Pearl and Snow Roads. Students were graded in all the subjects as well as days absent and tardy, much like they are today. This student received good grades, thereby promoting him to sixth grade for the next school year. (Courtesy of Ruth Fay.)

PEARL ROAD SCHOOL. When Pearl Road School opened in 1921, it was the end of one-room schoolhouses in Parma. Winifred Stroud served as the school's first principal. Pearl Road School was one of a few schools built around this time that were located in such a way that they were to face the main road as well as be a reasonable distance from the road in order to avoid dust and noise. (Courtesy of Parma Heights Historical Society.)

THOREAU PARK ELEMENTARY SCHOOL, 1930. Thoreau Park Elementary School was built in 1926 when Parma was a village. The school started with half-day sessions for grades kindergarten through sixth and shared the school with older grades until Schaaf Junior High School opened in 1928. After Schaaf opened, the primary grades went back to full-day classes. The first principals of Thoreau Park School were Mrs. McCreary and Mrs. Bardsalls. McCreary stayed on as principal and retired in 1944. (Courtesy of Cleveland Press Collection.)

SCHAAF JUNIOR HIGH SCHOOL. Schaaf Junior High was built at a time when Parma was a village, and the increasing number of children caused the school to be opened in 1928. Schaaf Junior High was eventually sold to a church group who later sold it to the City of Parma. The city then sold the building to Constellation Charter School. This is the Parma basketball team for Schaaf Junior High School in 1932. The members of this team won 12 out of 13 games played. Seen here are, from left to right, (first row) Jesse Beavon, Walter Routledge, Mike Kosarko, George Rees, Marlin Schultz, Emil Giorgione, Robert Heppler, Calvin Harmon, and E. O. Bartlow; (second row) George Frank, Joe Loas, Ralph Rodusky, William Skubovious, Ralph Forestek, and Nicholas Mindek; (third row) John Mikulka, Mike Petruziello, Paul Becker, John Janusczok, and Arthur Davis. (Courtesy of Cleveland Press Collection.)

ST. CHARLES SCHOOL, 1928. St. Charles School, part of St. Charles Borromeo Church, got its start in 1924 as a two-room school. Many parishes at the time built temporary churches so they could put more resources toward building parish schools. Two classrooms were added to the back of the frame church behind the sanctuary. Ground was broken for the school shown in this image on September 6, 1927. (Courtesy of Cleveland Press Collection.)

ST. CHARLES SCHOOL CLASS PHOTOGRAPH. Pictured here are students from the 1924–1925 class for St. Charles School. The school started out with 67 students and by 1925 had increased to 141 students. Fr. Nicholas Monaghan is shown with the fourth-, fifth-, and sixth-grade classes who all had class in one room at the time. (Courtesy of Parma Area Historical Society.)

STATE ROAD SCHOOL, 1951. State Road School, located on State Road, was built in 1921 at the same time as Pearl Road School and Ridge Road School. The three schools were considered sister schools back then because they were designed very similarly to one another. They all had nearly the same exteriors as well as a red brick floor on the inside, which State Road School still has today. Ridge Road School was located at Ridge Road and Day Drive and closed in 1962. (Courtesy of Mayor James W. Day.)

PARMA SENIOR HIGH SCHOOL, 1954. Parma Senior High School was built in 1953. It was originally designed for 2,000 students but soon had over 4,000 students, which gave it the title of being the largest school in Ohio at one time. Parma Senior High was the first school built in Parma after 22 years. (Courtesy of Cleveland Press Collection.)

NORMANDY HIGH SCHOOL. This image, taken in 1970, shows Normandy High School. Located on Pleasant Valley Road, it opened in 1968. This school was the Parma school system's third high school. Normandy started out with junior and senior grades and then added more grades in later years. The school is home to the Normandy Invaders. (Courtesy of the Cleveland Press Collection.)

PADUA FRANCISCAN HIGH SCHOOL. Currently the second-largest Catholic high school in northeast Ohio, Padua was founded by the Franciscan Province of the Sacred Heart of Saint Louis, Missouri, in 1961 as a school for boys. It became co-educational in 1983 and bases its teachings on the life and spirituality of Saint Francis of Assisi. (Courtesy of Mayor James W. Day.)

BYERS FIELD, 1950. In the early 1950s, a new football stadium for Parma Senior High was built at the site of a previous project abandoned in 1935. The field was reconditioned, with lights installed for nighttime football. The stadium, now called Byers Field after Superintendent Carl Byers, is located at Ridge Road and Ridgewood Drive and is one of the largest stadiums in Cuyahoga County. Prior to being a stadium, the area was once an apple orchard. (Courtesy of Cleveland Press Collection.)

SPLIT SESSIONS BEGIN, FEBRUARY 1977. Students of Parma's John Muir Elementary School (built in 1930) board buses to be transferred to John Glenn Elementary School in Seven Hills. In order to conserve natural gas, Parma had to close 14 of their 30 schools. The transferred students had to endure split sessions at school until March of that year. (Courtesy of Cleveland Press Collection.)

PARMA SOUTH PRESBYTERIAN CHURCH. This church was formed as the result of a merger of Parma Presbyterian and South Presbyterian Churches. Parma Presbyterian Church was organized in 1835 as a Congregational church but became Presbyterian in 1874. The South Presbyterian Church began in 1892 and met in a funeral home at the time. Because membership declined rapidly in 1935, South Presbyterian merged with Parma Presbyterian to form the Parma South Presbyterian Church. The current church was built in 1951 to accommodate its large membership. This church is located on Pearl Road in what is now Parma Heights. (Both courtesy of Cleveland Press Collection.)

St. Paul United Church of Christ, 1938. Officially organized in the fall of 1858, earlier history shows that in 1852 a small group of German farming families would sometimes meet in a small building at Pleasant Valley and York Roads to attend worship services. This photograph shows St. Paul's second church, which was built in 1915. (Courtesy of Cleveland Press Collection.)

St. Paul Church, Old and New. This picture was taken sometime around 1960 when the new church (shown in the background) was built. The second church (pictured front right) was built in 1915 but had to be torn down when the road was widened. The church in the background is the current church today. (Courtesy of St. Paul United Church of Christ.)

HOLY FAMILY CATHOLIC CHURCH. Holy Family Catholic Church received its start in 1872 when religious services were held at a Parma home and conducted by Rev. Father Quigley. The first church opened in 1873 and was the main church until 1911, when a larger red brick church was built. The 1942 image above shows the second church of Holy Family. Their current church, pictured below in 1974, has been the fourth church of Holy Family since 1965, when a new building needed to be constructed as the parish began to grow. (Both courtesy of Cleveland Press Collection.)

St. Peter United Church of Christ.
St. Peter Church was founded in 1858 by a group of German settlers. The image above shows the parsonage, built in 1886, which is still standing on Broadview Road. In 1958, the church moved to a new location around the corner from this house and is now located in Seven Hills. Behind the parsonage is a cemetery belonging to St. Peter Church that has graves dating back to the early 1800s. St. Peter United Church of Christ recently celebrated its 150th anniversary in 2008. The image to the left is that of St. Peter's first church on Broadview Road. (Above, courtesy of Susan Eid; at left, Parma Area Historical Society.)

BETHLEHEM LUTHERAN CHURCH. The Bethlehem Lutheran Church was established in the early 1900s when families from St. Mark Lutheran Church in Cleveland joined together. The first building was on the corner of State and Pleasant Valley Roads, and the first religious service took place on November 13, 1904. The current building on State Road was constructed in the 1960s, just south of the original location. (Courtesy of Susan Eid.)

ST. CHARLES BORROMEO CHURCH, 1955. A temporary frame church was built in 1923 so that more funding could be used toward building a school. Starting out with 13 families in April 1923, the church grew to 90 families by 1924. The frame church cost $5,000 to build and stood where the St. Charles Corrigan Gym is currently. In 1953, ground was broken for a new church, and the first mass was held on Easter Sunday in 1955. (Courtesy of Cleveland Press Collection.)

BETHANY EVANGELICAL LUTHERAN CHURCH, 1951. This church got its start in 1922 when four men and eight women, along with 12 children, started a service together in the room of a house at Pearl and Ridge Roads. In 1926, a lot was purchased at 5994 Ridge Road in which to build a chapel. By the end of that year, the cornerstone was set for the new unfinished church. In May 1927, the church was dedicated. (Courtesy of Cleveland Public Library Photograph Collection/ James Thomas.)

GOOD SHEPHERD UNITED METHODIST CHURCH. This church received its start in 1926 and was originally named the First United Brethren in Christ Church of Parma. The congregation first met in an old schoolhouse, and when it was sold at auction the current property at State Road for the church was purchased. The building was dedicated in May 1930. (Courtesy of Susan Eid.)

RIDGE ROAD UNITED CHURCH OF CHRIST. The first worship service took place in Parma Community Hall on September 27, 1927. Soon a lot was purchased, and in October 1932, a new church was dedicated. As membership continued to grow, the church was torn down in 1962 to make way for a new church structure. (Courtesy of Susan Eid.)

RIDGEWOOD UNITED METHODIST CHURCH. This church was dedicated at its current location on Ridge Road on May 12, 1929. At the time of this picture, the congregation was worshiping in the basement where the original church was located. In 1951, a second section was added onto the sanctuary, and in 1958 the classroom additions were completed. The stained-glass windows, added to the sanctuary in 1980, tell the history of the church. Currently there are over 700 members. (Courtesy of Cleveland Press Collection.)

St. Francis de Sales. Bishop Joseph Schrembs established this church on July 9, 1931. In the early years, Pastor Francis J. McGlynn conducted mass in the auditorium of John Muir Elementary School or at the Parmadale Orphanage. Father McGlynn eventually collected enough money to buy land for the first church, which was dedicated on May 19, 1935. (Courtesy of Kathleen Schmidt.)

Parma Lutheran Church. Located at 5280 Broadview Road, this church got its start in 1932 at a storefront on State Road. The first worship service was held on October 20, 1932, with 37 members attending. Three months later, in 1933, the congregation was organized and the chapel was dedicated. Clarence Weiss was the first pastor. Shown here in 1939 are workers constructing the building. (Courtesy of Cleveland Press Collection.)

Three

PARMA'S FINEST

The Parma Police Department was organized in 1925 after Parma became a village. The first location of the department was in the basement of the old town hall at Ridge Road and Bean Road (now Ridgewood Drive). The policemen shared space with the fire department that had been established one year earlier. Before that, constables were the main peacekeepers around the township. Once the police force became organized, the department consisted of one marshal and two deputy marshals. The men were required to supply their own equipment. By 1932, the city grew to have seven policemen on the force. In 1934, the police and fire departments moved to the fire station on Snow Road and Dresden Avenue. Because of the rapid growth of Parma, the police department was then moved to its own facility on West Fifty-fourth Street in 1953. In 2000, the police department moved yet again to its current location on Powers Boulevard. Today the department currently includes the chief of police, four captains, five lieutenants, nine sergeants, over 50 patrol officers, and 10 detectives.

Before the fire department was organized, fires were usually put out by neighbors in a bucket brigade. Established in 1924, the fire department required members to supply their own equipment. The three firefighters of this time received $100 a month for working 24 hours a day, seven days a week, with one day off per month. When on duty, they slept in a jail cell in the town hall. Since then, the fire department has grown and currently has five fire stations located around the city. The first fire station building was on Snow Road and is still there now but currently unoccupied. The five stations in the city are located on Snow Road, State Road, Ridge Road, and two on Pleasant Valley Road. This chapter features many of the early policemen and firefighters that have served the city over the years.

PARMA POLICEMEN. Having to work alongside the fire department in the basement of the old town hall, it soon became cramped. In 1934, the police headquarters was moved to the first fire station on Snow Road, where it continued to share space with the fire department, but this time with much more room. (Courtesy of Parma Police Department.)

PARMA POLICE, 1929. Pictured here are Parma police next to the new police cars. They are, from left to right, (first row) John J. Hajek, Harvey Wagner, Charles Tesar, Lester Roeper, and Asa Volkman; (second row) Harry Burkle, Herbert Tiliske, Walter Meese, Richard Rupp, and Willis Veran; the child in front is Don Roeper. (Courtesy of Parma Police Department.)

POLICE VEHICLES. In 1945, under Chief Lester Roeper, the Detective Bureau was established in order to satisfy the need for specialization. This image shows the 1953 Fords and was taken on Ridge Road at the old police station on West 54th Street. (Courtesy of Parma Police Department.)

PARMA POLICE C. 1930. Parma policemen take the time to pose for a picture with their new cruisers and motorcycles. They are standing in front of the old fire station on Snow Road, which is no longer in use. (Courtesy of Parma Police Department.)

POLICE POSITIONS. In 1932, a new ordinance replaced the title of deputy marshal with the position of patrolman. Their salaries were as follows: patrolman first grade, $1,800 per year; patrolman second grade, $1,700 per year; patrolman third grade, $1,600 per year. (Courtesy of Parma Police Department.)

POLICE MOTORCYCLES. This photograph, taken around 1942, shows patrolman Paul Ranker and Sgt. Lester Roeper showing off the department's new motorcycles. The bikes were a more inexpensive method of transportation that allowed for faster travel throughout the city, primarily for the enforcement of traffic laws. (Courtesy of Parma Police Department.)

POLICE STATION, 1953. In 1953, a new police station opened at 5750 West Fifty-fourth Street. This was the third location the police department had been housed in since it was organized in 1925. This building was demolished when the new Parma Justice Center opened in 2000 on Powers Boulevard. (Courtesy of Cleveland Press Collection.)

POLICE CHIEF. Shown here is Parma police chief Garry Burczyk in 1932. Around 1936, the newspapers boasted about Parma's police officers conducting a raid and catching a liquor bootlegger. That same year, patrolman Walter Meese single-handedly caught two robbers who had escaped from a penitentiary in Illinois. (Courtesy of Parma Area Historical Society.)

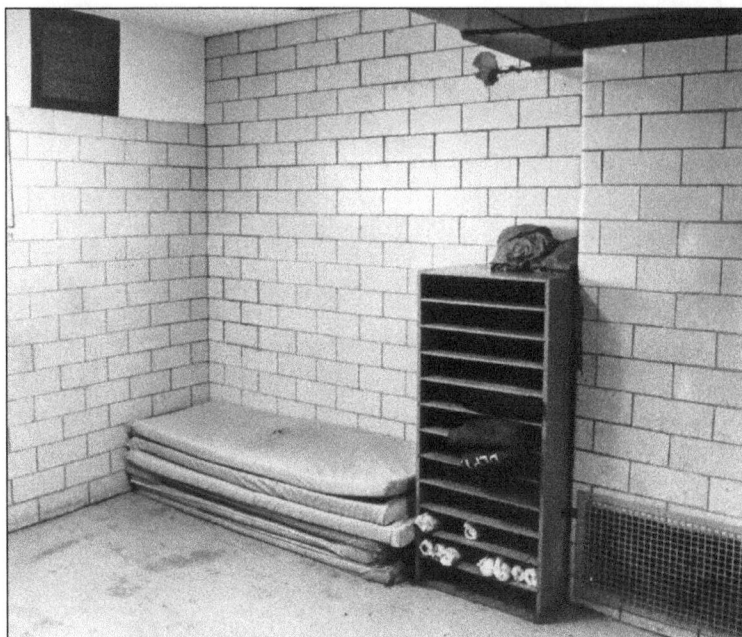

JAILHOUSE. The old adage of receiving bread and water in prison held true in the early 1800s. Back then, a prisoner was lucky to have a bed, which was usually made out of wood. Shown here in 1975 is the men's detention area at the Parma Jail on West Fifty-fourth Street. Criminals were often detained in this holding cell temporarily until further processing. (Courtesy of Cleveland Press Collection.)

THE CONVERTIBLE AMBULANCE. This 1936 Plymouth was the new vehicle for the police department. It was a combination squad car and ambulance and thought to be the only one of its kind in the nation during that time. (Courtesy of Cuyahoga County Library Parma-South Branch.)

LOST BOY. Taken in May 1930, patrolman Walter Fanta holds a lost three-year-old boy that was found at Pearl and Ridge Roads. A newspaper article at the time said that kids seemed to flock to the officer because he bought them ice cream cones. The lost boy was shortly reunited with his parents. (Courtesy of Cleveland Press Collection.)

DEACONESS ENTRANCE. Shown here in 1938 are Parma policemen at Deaconess Hospital. They are standing near the old emergency entrance. Pictured among the group is Lester Roeper. Deaconess Hospital was established in 1920 and started out by converting a house into a 28-bed hospital. Because of its success, a new structure was built in 1928. (Courtesy of Parma Area Historical Society.)

PARMA POLICEMEN, 1938. The Parma Police Pistol Club poses for a photograph. Seen here are, from left to right, (first row) Sgt. Harvey Wagner, patrolmen James Flahan, Walter Meese, Chief Garry Burczyk, patrolman J. Gaughan, and Sgt. Lester Roeper; (second row) patrolmen Asa Volkman, Peter Cudlin, Paul Reinker, Capt. Herbert Tiliske, patrolman Edwin Speller, and Sgt. Harry Burkle. (Courtesy of Cleveland Public Library Photograph Collection/*Cleveland News.*)

TRAFFIC SIGNS, 1942. Parma police show their support for the victory speed limit of 35 miles per hour. The Ohio Highway Department placed 1,600 of these signs around the state of Ohio to remind motorists of the speed limit. Pictured here are patrolmen Costley and Meese. (Courtesy of Cleveland Press Collection.)

NEW POLICE EMBLEM, 1961. The police department was on the search for a new police emblem. They decided to hold a contest conducted at Parma Senior High School, and the winner would have his or her design displayed on all Parma Police cruisers. Lesley Lewand, a 17-year-old senior, was declared the winner and is shown holding the winning design. Seen here are, from left to right, Chief Francis N. Szabo, patrolman William Nickels, winner Lewand, and runners-up Bruce Boyle and Carol Hotaling. (Courtesy of Cleveland Press Collection.)

PARMA POLICE CARS, 1978. The police department purchased new vehicles in 1978. This image shows the 17 white Chevrolet Impalas that were bought for $136,984. At the time of this photograph, equipment was being transferred into the new cars in order for them to be ready to patrol the streets. (Courtesy of Cleveland Press Collection.)

GERMAN CENTRAL FARM, 1942. The chief of police investigates vandalism at the German Central Farm. At that time, the United States was fighting the Germans in World War II. Vandals broke out windows, and the chief is pictured here holding a broken plate of glass while he checks out the surroundings. (Courtesy of Cleveland Press Collection.)

PARMA PATROLMEN. Pictured here in 1969 are, from left to right, Richard Becker, Nick Pastura, Dennis Deluca, and Mark Mabry. During the mid-1800s, early bulletproof vests were made out of many layers of cotton. In the late 1960s, a company manufactured vests from quilted nylon and steel plates. These "barrier vests" were the first widely used police vests for law enforcement. (Courtesy of Cleveland Press Collection.)

FIRE STATION, 1930. In 1925, the fire and police departments shared the same quarters in the basement of the town hall. In 1934, the police headquarters was moved to this fire station at Snow Road and Dresden Avenue, again sharing facilities with the fire department until a separate location was built for the police on West Fifty-Fourth Street. (Courtesy of Cleveland Press Collection.)

FIRE STATION, 1950. Early firefighters had no protection against smoke inhalation, so they often grew beards, and when fighting a fire they would soak their beards in water, bite the ends, and breathe through them when the area became filled with smoke. While this did not completely solve the problem, it helped to filter some of the smoke. (Courtesy of Cleveland Press Collection.)

PARMA FIREMEN. Shown here in 1926 are, from left to right, Lt. Thomas Daugherty, Harry Aves, Otto Mezera, and Charles Mandley. In the 1920s, the Parma Village Fire Department proudly claimed that they could be ready to go in 45 seconds after receiving a call. (Courtesy of Cleveland Press Collection.)

RESCUE. This image, taken in 1939, shows Parma firemen after they rescued boys that had fallen through the ice. From left to right are Edward Zeeck, William O'Connell, and Captain Clyde Jones. Early firefighters had no formal training like there is today. They were usually taught by their elders. (Courtesy of Cleveland Press Collection.)

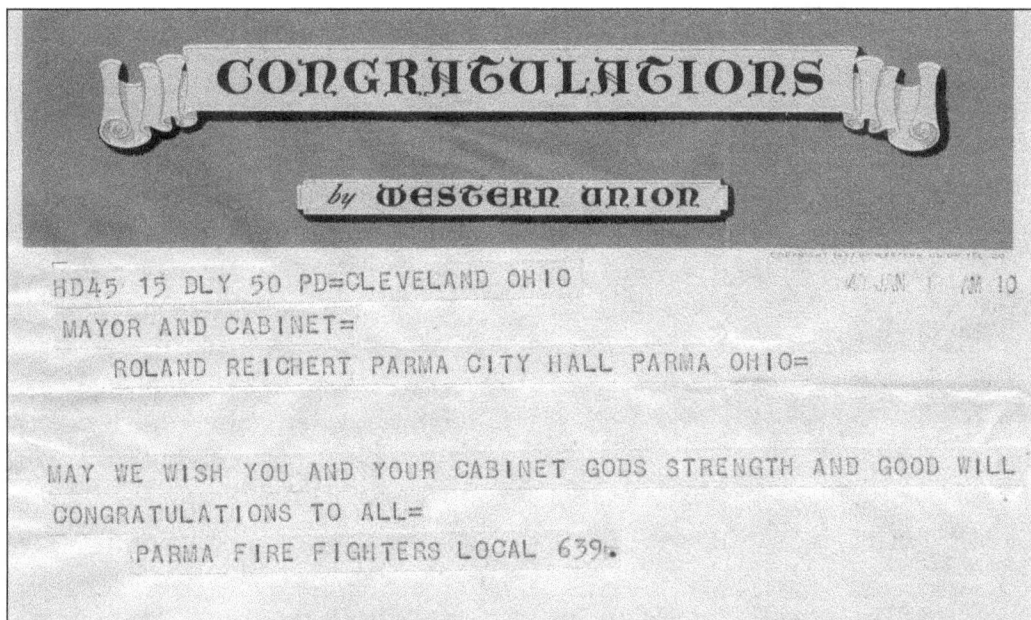

CONGRATULATIONS.

by WESTERN UNION

HD45 15 DLY 50 PD=CLEVELAND OHIO   4 JAN 1 M 10

MAYOR AND CABINET=

ROLAND REICHERT PARMA CITY HALL PARMA OHIO=

MAY WE WISH YOU AND YOUR CABINET GODS STRENGTH AND GOOD WILL

CONGRATULATIONS TO ALL=

PARMA FIRE FIGHTERS LOCAL 639.

CONGRATULATIONS. This Western Union telegram, dated January 1, 1940, was sent by the Parma firefighters to Mayor Roland Reichert and his cabinet. Reichert served as mayor of Parma from 1936 to 1942. He was called away to the service and afterwards resumed his position again from 1946 to 1949. (Courtesy of Cuyahoga County Library Parma-South Branch.)

AMERICAN LAFRANCE, 1924. Shown here in 1928 are, from left to right, Harry Aves, William O'Connell, Thomas Daugherty, Clyde Jones, and unidentified. Records show that in the mid-1700s early fire helmets were made out of leather. In the 1830s, a helmet was designed that is similar to the traditional one used today. (Courtesy of Cleveland Press Collection.)

PARMA FIRE DEPARTMENT. Pictured in 1960 admiring the newly purchased ladder truck are, from left to right, Minor George, Mayor Sylvester Augustine, and fire chief Robert Koch. In the 1960s, Parma's population was rapidly growing, prompting the city to add two new fire stations. (Courtesy of Cleveland Press Collection.)

PARMA DRILL. Shown here in 1940 are Parma firemen conducting a fire drill at Evergreen Lake off of Pearl Road. Early equipment included hand pumpers, which required a person to pump the device up and down rapidly in order to get water out. While this method made a person easily tired, it became much more effective than the bucket brigades previously used. (Courtesy of Parma Area Historical Society.)

Four

INDUSTRY AND BUSINESSES

Parma's early beginnings were primarily agricultural. As more settlers arrived, many farms were built in the area. The settlers grew crops in order to sell them or to provide for their families. Over time, Parma's agricultural industry made way for manufacturing, and thus Parma's manufacturing industry has greatly expanded over the years. The city got its business start in the mid-1800s with William and Dudley Humphrey, who were two of Parma's earliest businessmen. William and Dudley arrived from Connecticut and brought with them their skills in making clocks by opening a clock business in Parma. They remained in business from 1836 to 1851. Since the start of this early business, Parma has grown quickly in over 150 years. In 1970, Parma's population reached almost 100,000, which caused major businesses and corporations to locate themselves in the city to keep up with the growing demand for products and services. This not only provided jobs to many residents in Parma, it helped make it one of the largest cities in Cuyahoga County.

From the corner bakery down the street to the huge corporation across town, Parma has had many businesses that vastly serve different functions to accommodate its residents, which also help to diversify the city. While some businesses have not stood the test of time, they have definitely left a mark on the city that inspired it to grow and be more prosperous. Today Parma boasts major businesses in the automotive, medical, and educational areas. It is home to certain establishments such as the General Motors Chevrolet Plant, Parma Community General Hospital, and Cuyahoga Community College. This chapter highlights only a few of the many businesses that are in the area. While many stores have come and gone, their memories have left a lasting impression on the residents of this city.

FROELICH'S STORE. Before Parma became a village, it was part of Brooklyn Township. This image, from 1892, shows Froelich's Store located in the Parma area that was previously Brooklyn Township. Shown here are, from left to right, Elsie Froelich, Jake Buhl, and Louis Dentzer. (Courtesy of Parma Area Historical Society.)

PARMA DAIRY. This is an early Parma milk delivery service. Pictured is Reinhart Schultz delivering milk in his horse-drawn buggy. Schultz was the father of schoolteacher Thelma Schultz. He owned a 9-acre farm where Pearl Road School now stands in Parma Heights. Milk was usually delivered in the mornings when the weather outside was still cool. (Courtesy of Parma Heights Historical Society.)

WALTER ICE COMPANY. Shown here is the Walter Ice Company truck fleet in 1934. Roy Walter, also known as the "Iceman," was born in Parma in 1895. In the back of his land there was a pond, and in the winter when it froze he would cut sections of the ice with handsaws and float these sections onto an elevator ramp. They were then chipped into smaller pieces and sold. (Courtesy of Parma Area Historical Society.)

BUILDINGS AT CRILE HOSPITAL. Crile Hospital was built in May of 1943 by the U.S. Army for soldiers and veterans. It was dedicated on March 31, 1944, and the first patients arrived on April 8, 1944. It was located on York Road, where Cuyahoga Community College now stands. The hospital was named in honor of Col. George W. Crile Sr. and had 108 beds within 83 buildings. The hospital closed its doors in 1964. (Courtesy of Mayor James W. Day.)

NIKE MISSILE SITE. In 1956, a Nike missile site was added to the grounds of Crile Hospital as part of the nation's general defense program. There were seven sites built around Cuyahoga County. Each site contained Nike-Ajax missiles, a generator, underground missile storage and launchers, a fueling area, and barracks. The Parma-Parma Heights base was located at 11000 York Road. It later became the site of Cuyahoga Community College's Western Campus. (Courtesy of Ron Bissell.)

PARMA CHEVROLET PLANT, C. 1949. Shown here is the new General Motors Chevrolet Plant under construction. General Motors opened this plant at Brookpark and Stumph Roads. It was originally put into service to build automatic transmissions. In later years of manufacturing, the company expanded its operation to include additional parts for various vehicles. (Courtesy of Mayor James W. Day.)

GENERAL MOTORS CHEVROLET PLANT. The Chevrolet plant was built after World War II as part of the General Motors expansion plan. Construction on the plant started in 1947 with an estimated cost of $7.5 million. In 1949, the plant opened, and production of pressed-metal parts and Powerglide transmissions began. The image above shows the Chevrolet plant in 1969, while the picture below shows a full employee parking lot in 1974. General Motors chose Parma for the site of the plant because of its central location as well as the area's shipping facilities and labor. (Both courtesy of Cleveland Press Collection.)

CHEVROLET PLANT AERIAL VIEW, 1950. During the 1960s, General Motors was one of Parma's leading industrial employers. This large plant spanned 291 acres, and the General Motors Training Center, 1 of 30 in the nation at the time, was located across the street. (Courtesy of Cleveland Press Collection.)

ASSEMBLY LINE. Pictured here in 1950 are the men of the Chevrolet plant assembling the new Powerglide automatic transmissions. The Powerglide was a two-speed automatic transmission and was available in Chevrolet automobiles from 1950 to the early 1970s. (Courtesy of Cleveland Press Collection.)

CHEVROLET WORKERS, 1964.
By 1956, the plant employed
7,600 people and rose to 7,740
in 1963. A recession during
the 1980s caused the plant to
reduce its employees to 3,600.
Currently the plant employs
about 1,000 people. In 1979,
the 25 millionth transmission
was made. Transmissions were
being assembled in Parma
until 1986. (Courtesy of
Cleveland Press Collection.)

**GENERAL MOTORS, APRIL
1953.** Shown here are women
at the General Motors plant
in Parma assembling gears
for Chevrolet's Powerglide
automatic transmission. Of
the 7,500 employees working
during this time, over 1,000
were women. (Courtesy of
Cleveland Press Collection.)

PARMATOWN MALL. Parmatown Mall was built in 1956 as a shopping plaza and later became enclosed in the 1960s. Around 1968, there were over 100 stores in the mall, such as Miller Drugs, Paris Hats, Pick-N-Pay, Acme Meats, Kitchen Maid Meats, Kurtz Furniture, and Rosenblum's among many more. (Courtesy of Mayor James W. Day.)

PARMATOWN GROUND-BREAKING. Shown here in 1959 is the ground-breaking ceremony for Parmatown Mall when it was becoming enclosed. Handling the spades are, from left to right, N. L. Dauby, David Geller, James W. Day, Francis A. Coy, Sam Miller, Arthur Begam, Mayor Joseph Kader, and Sam Rosenberg. (Courtesy of Cleveland Press Collection.)

Higbee's Store Ground-Breaking, 1966. Parma mayor James W. Day (left), Higbee's board chairman John P. Murphy (center), and Forest City Material Company president Max Ratner are at the ground-breaking ceremonies for the new Higbee's store at Parmatown Mall. The 185,000-square-foot Higbee Store opened in 1966. Located at the west end of the mall, it planned to employ 400 people, most of them residents of the city. (Courtesy of Cleveland Press Collection.)

Winkelmans, 1968. Winkelmans was a high-end department store for women located inside Parmatown Mall. The mall had a variety of stores in order to satisfy the growing population emerging at the time. (Courtesy of Cleveland Press Collection.)

TRAINING DAY AT MAY COMPANY, 1960. The May Company Department store opened its doors at Parmatown Mall in 1960. The training director of May Company at Parmatown Mall, Jacqueline Lyons (far right), teaches new trainees how to use the cash register. Note the size and bulkiness of the cash register, which is quite large compared to the technology used today. As well as bringing business to the area, Parmatown Mall also gave jobs to many area residents. The trainees are, from left to right, Leona Rygielski, Pat Oberst, Marie Paine, and Margaret Rots. (Courtesy of Cleveland Press Collection.)

CHRISTMASTIME AT PARMATOWN MALL. A massive Santa Claus, measuring between 20 and 25 feet, was displayed on the grounds of the May Company entrance at the mall in 1960. This jolly giant Santa was used to attract customers to the joys of shopping at Christmas. (Courtesy of Cleveland Press Collection.)

SANTA CLAUS CASTLE. Pictured here in 1961 is the Santa Claus castle at Parmatown Mall in front of the S. S. Kresge store. The castle was 30 feet high and topped with a bell tower. The inside of this pink, blue, and white castle was heated, and it also had a red and gold throne for Santa. Santa was giving out coloring books that year to young children visiting him. (Courtesy of Cleveland Press Collection.)

PARMATOWN STRIP, 1961. Around this time, Parmatown added a mall wing addition to the property. The new wing had stores grouped in four buildings and provided spacious garden-type shopping. Only 40 acres were built on, which left plenty of room for the mall to expand on the 114-acre property. (Courtesy of Cleveland Press Collection.)

THE HEART OF PARMA. Pictured here in 1969 are three important buildings in Parma. The L-shaped structure in the upper left is city hall. Parma Community General Hospital is in the center right, and the Parma School Administration building is in the lower left corner. (Courtesy of Cleveland Press Collection.)

FISHER FOODS, 1960. This photograph was taken in front of Fisher Foods, a grocery store at the time. It was located in a strip in front of Parmatown Mall. In the 1960s, more than 50,000 people shopped at Parmatown Mall each week, which caused the area to expand as demand grew. While this outdoor shopping center opened in 1956, a few others soon followed. Pleasant Valley and Snowville opened in 1958, and Midtown Plaza was built in 1960. (Courtesy of Cleveland Press Collection.)

PARMA BUSINESSES. Shown here in 1962 are Parma Community General Hospital (center left), city hall, and Parmatown (upper left). At the top of the image lies Ridgewood Lake. Parma was growing quickly during this time as businesses and buildings started appearing everywhere. (Courtesy of Cleveland Press Collection.)

PARMA COMMUNITY GENERAL HOSPITAL, 1961. In 1957, a committee started a fund-raising drive to raise money for the proposed hospital. In August 1961, the hospital opened its doors. In 2000, Parma Community General Hospital was named one of the top 100 hospitals in the country by Healthcare Industries Association and the Health Network. (Courtesy of Cleveland Press Collection.)

BRINGING OUT THE SHOVELS. This image shows the ground-breaking ceremony at the future site of Parma Community General Hospital in September 1958. Pictured here are mayors from Parma Heights, Seven Hills, North Royalton, Brooklyn, and Brooklyn Heights, along with Mayor James W. Day of Parma. Mayor Day served as mayor of Parma from 1962 to 1967. (Courtesy of Cleveland Press Collection.)

A COLLEGE WITHIN A PARK. That was the nickname given to the Cuyahoga Community College's western campus. This aerial view depicts buildings of Crile Hospital that were in the process of being torn down to make way for the campus. The trees were preserved and were considered the main feature of the campus. (Courtesy of Cleveland Press Collection.)

TRI-C. The college opened in September of 1966 with 2,600 students enrolled. In October 1996, Pres. Bill Clinton visited the campus and talked to a crowd of 15,000 people about education. Clinton had previously visited Cleveland and made sure to stop at Parma Pierogies restaurant before going on his way. (Courtesy of Cleveland Press Collection.)

CUYAHOGA COMMUNITY COLLEGE, 1975. This 200-acre setting includes Veterans Memorial Garden, as well as many streams, ponds, and fountains. When Crile Hospital announced that it was closing its doors, speculation arose as to what would take its place. Many thought it might become a state park, veterans' cemetery, or even a mental hospital. (Courtesy of Cleveland Press Collection.)

INSIDE THE GALLERIA AT CUYAHOGA COMMUNITY COLLEGE, 1975. The galleria at the college offers a cafeteria, library, snack bar, student lounges, study areas, bookstore, game room, and conference rooms. This allows students to have a place to study or relax in between classes. (Courtesy of Cleveland Press Collection.)

HOLY FAMILY HOME. In 1956, the Holy Family Home was established by the Dominican Sisters of Hawthorne, New York, who cared for cancer patients. A prominent figure in the development of the home was Rose Hawthorne, daughter of writer Nathaniel Hawthorne. Holy Family Home has taken care of over 12,000 patients with cancer at no cost. (Courtesy of Mayor James W. Day.)

MODERN TOOL AND DIE, 1960. This view from the air shows the intersection of West 130th Street and Brookpark Road. Modern Tool and Die, located at the top left corner, was a major industrial employer and made metal stampings, tools, and dies. It was founded in 1931 by Ted Moll and was a family-owned private company. It was originally known as the Western Stamping and Manufacturing Company. Parma Lumber, another local area business, can also be seen in this picture. West 130th Street was originally known as Settlement Road. (Courtesy of Cleveland Press Collection.)

RIDGEWOOD GOLF COURSE, 1927. Ridgewood Golf Course opened in 1925 and was built by Howard A. Stahl's company. It was designed by Grange Alves, who once owned a driving range near Euclid Beach Park. In order to get the course ready each year, preseason chores included rolling the fairways, mowing and fertilizing the greens and tees, replacing bridges, and planting trees. (Courtesy of Cleveland Press Collection.)

FAMOUS GOLFERS. Ridgewood has had some golf greats play on its course. In 1926, the Ohio Public Links was played there. Golfers such as Babe Didrikson, Walter Hagen, Byron Nelson, Billie Burke, Harry Rees, and Arnold Palmer also competed at Ridgewood. Rees was the club professional and gave lessons to golfers. (Courtesy of Cleveland Press Collection.)

RIDGEWOOD GOLF GAME. Taken at the No. 7 hole in 1939 are Art Behm, Al Leach, John Skinner, Ken Graves, Bill Burke, Harry Rees, Carl Ramser, Byron Nelson, and Walter Hagen (spelled incorrectly in the image). The toughest hole at the time was No. 2, which was a 435-yard backbreaker. The hole was a par four. (Courtesy of Councilman Ken Ramser.)

COWGILL PRINTING. In 1927, Howard Cowgill started a printing company in his basement on Arithmere Avenue in Old Brooklyn. Later on he moved his business into a three-car garage on Russell Avenue in Parma. It remained there until 1949, when Cowgill constructed the new building now located on Brookpark Road in Parma. This image, taken in the early 1960s, shows Nick Chychlyk working on expanding the building. (Courtesy of Cowgill Printing Company.)

COWGILL BUILDING EXPANSION, 1960s. Cowgill Printing is still family owned and operated. It is considered Parma's oldest established business. From left to right are unidentified, Bob Weatherby, Gordon Cowgill, Jim Dancick, Bill Sevcheck, unidentified, Jake Leiby, and Nick Chychlyk. (Courtesy of Cowgill Printing Company.)

OVERHEAD VIEW OF PARMADALE, 1935. In 1925, a new type of village was created—this one for children. Parmadale Children's Village of St. Vincent de Paul provided homes for the needy and poor children of Cleveland. This structure housed 360 boys and spanned 180 acres of land on State Road. Parmadale consisted of small cottage-type buildings and was the first Catholic children's village. Today Parmadale helps youth deal with trauma or other developmental disabilities. (Courtesy of Cleveland Press Collection.)

PARMADALE DORMITORIES, 1930. When Parmadale first opened, it consisted of 12 cottages, a dining hall, school, chapel, and power plant. Parmadale housed 500 boys from various orphanages. There were 40 boys to each cottage, and each cottage was supervised by two nuns at the time. In 1947, girls were transferred to Parmadale. (Courtesy of Cleveland Press Collection.)

PARMADALE AERIAL. The average age of a Parmadale boy was seven years old. The children lived in cottage-type houses that resembled a homelike atmosphere. They often participated in many outings and were taken to events happening around Cleveland. Shown here is Parmadale in 1936. (Courtesy of Cleveland Press Collection.)

SIEBOLD'S MARKET. This advertisement for Siebold's Market appeared in 1948 in the *Parma Post.* Located at 5344 State Road, it was a grocery store as well as a meat market. Siebold's Market is no longer there, but it was located in the area now known as Ukrainian Village, which was dedicated in 2009 and includes a 2-mile stretch of State Road. The village features two Ukrainian churches and many Ukrainian-owned businesses. (Courtesy of Councilman Ken Ramser.)

SIEBOLD'S MARKET

5344-46 State Road   **FLorida 1622**

Specials for This Week-End Only!

Grocery Specials	Meat Specials

NO. 2 CAN
Grapefr. Juice 3 for **25c**
APPLE OR GRAPE
Jelly Jar **25c**
FRESH GROUND
Bob White Coffee Lb. **41c**
Applesauce 2 for **25c**
Eating Apples 2 lbs. **23c**
FROZEN WHOLE
Strawberries 45c

FRESH BOSTON BUTT
Pork Roast Lb. **57c**
FRESH GROUND
Beef Lb. **49c**
FRESH STEER
Beef Liver Lb. **59c**
SWIFT SELECT — SHORT CUT
Standing Rib Lb. **69c**
WE SPECIALIZE IN SWIFT
PREMIUM AND SWIFT SELECT
BEEF, VEAL AND LAMB

WE DELIVER ANYWHERE

KADER'S for BARGAINS

See Joe and Andy   Firestone Products

We Save You Money on TIRES MAKE YOUR OWN TERMS

Outboard Motor 3.6 H.P. 89.85
De Luxe Electric Range 224.95
30-Gal. Automatic Water Tank 79.95
Hamilton Beach Mixer 17.95
Sunbeam Hedge Trimmer 37.50
Westinghouse Roaster 26.95

EASY TERMS
WE GIVE EAGLE STAMPS

SALE
Boys' and Girls'
Bicycles
$38.95 up

Fix Up The Outside!
HOUSE PAINT
24.95 gal.
Goes further, covers better, wears longer. Costs less because two coats do the work of three.

Firestone
HOUSE PAINT
Superior Quality

Sunfast Trim and Shutter
PAINT
7.29 gal.
Resists sun and weather. Non-fading brilliant colors.

Beautiful
SEAT COVERS
Quality Seat Covers Only
$5.95 Up

WE GIVE EAGLE STAMPS

KADER'S
HOME AND AUTO SUPPLY STORE
— PARMA —
SH. 1000   Open Eve. to 8 P.M.   5443 State Road

KADER'S APPLIANCE AND TIRE CENTER, 1958. Kader's was a business located on State Road and Brookview Boulevard. The store was owned by former mayor Joseph W. Kader, who served as mayor of Parma from 1958 to 1959. It got its start in 1937 as a two-pump gas station and then later turned into a hardware store in 1944. Before Kader's was built, a big garage was located there that showed movies every Saturday afternoon to the neighborhood children. Pictured at left is an advertisement for Kader's from a 1948 *Parma Post* newspaper. (Above, courtesy of Cleveland Press Collection; at left, Councilman Ken Ramser.)

PARMATOWN LANES, 1968. Parmatown Lanes opened in the season of 1959–1960 and was a favorite of many residents. Located on Day Drive, it had approximately 42 lanes. Television station WUAB got its start at a booth in Parmatown Lanes, where local celebrities such as Superhost often performed. Parmatown Lanes closed in the 1980s before it could celebrate its 25th anniversary. (Courtesy of Cleveland Press Collection.)

SIRL'S GARAGE, MID-1960S. Built in 1951, Sirl's Garage replaced the old gas station that had previously been there on York Road. Before that, Sirl's was on the site of Parma's first blacksmith shop, which opened in 1914 and was owned by Michael Sirl. It was later bought by Ralph Sirl in the 1940s. (Courtesy of Dale R. Sirl.)

PARMA THEATRE, JANUARY 1950. Opening on October 17, 1936, the first movie shown at the theater was *The Gorgeous Hussy*, starring Joan Crawford and Robert Taylor. It started as a single theater with about 1,500 seats before dividing into three to four screens in the late 1970s. Parma also had a drive-in theater located on Brookpark Road near the Chevrolet plant that closed around 1990. The city had another theater located inside Parmatown Mall that opened in 1967. Ticket prices to see a movie around that time were $2 for adults and 60¢ for children. Candy was available for 5¢ and popcorn was sold in a box for 15¢; soda was also available for 25¢. The Parmatown Mall Cinema closed its doors in 2004, but the Parma Theatre pictured here is still open. (Courtesy of Cleveland Press Collection.)

Five

ROADS AND TRANSPORTATION

Parma first started out with dirt roads that had been cut out from the woods. Soon after, wooden planks were laid across the dirt roads to prevent the paths from deteriorating in bad weather. In 1876, a plank toll road, the Brighton and Parma Plank Road (B&P), was built. This road extended from State Road on the south side to the intersection of York Road and Wooster Road (now Pearl Road). Toll roads were soon built to keep the roads in usable condition. Road companies put up tollgates and charged fees for using the roads. A tollbooth was located at the intersection of Olde York and Pearl Roads in what is now Parma Heights. A replica of the tollbooth now stands near the Parma Heights Library.

In the 1920s, a streetcar known as the "dinkey" was a major mode of transportation. In the late 1800s, A. C. Dinkey, an electrical engineer in Pittsburgh, designed an electric streetcar controller. This device enabled the motorman, when reaching the end of the line, to remove the control handle, lock the controller, and put the control handle on at the other end of the streetcar. This meant that the dinkey did not have to be turned around to head in the opposite direction. Passengers sometimes helped the operator switch handles on the streetcar.

The dinkey in Parma ran along State Road from Ridgewood Drive to Brookpark Road. It had often been described as moving like "a circus elephant waddling down the center of the street." The dinkey was also called the Toonerville Trolley, named after a popular comic strip at the time. Dinkey service started in 1915 and ended in 1939 when buses became an easier and faster form of transportation.

This chapter depicts earlier forms of travel as well as aerial views of the city at the time. These photographs also show how much the city has developed over the years.

Tollgate at York

TOLLBOOTH. This tollbooth was near the intersection of Olde York and Pearl Roads in what is now Parma Heights. Early residents remember being able to buy licorice and other candy at the tollbooth. For those using the road, the following charges applied: wagon with two horses, 10¢; stagecoach, 6¢; sleigh with one horse, 4¢; and bicycle, 4¢. (Courtesy of Parma Heights Historical Society.)

PARMA DINKEY. There were a few dinkeys that ran through Parma. One of them was No. 867 and called the State Road Dinkey. It ran every 30 minutes, and its highest year ever was in 1925 with 530,000 people having ridden the dinkey. Dinkey No. 867 was one of four that only had two doors. The rest had four doors. (Courtesy of Cleveland Press Collection.)

DINKEY NOS. 867 AND 48. Pictured here are Dinkey Nos. 867 and 48. While the State Road Dinkey ran every 30 minutes, a second car was added during rush hour to make the service run every 15 minutes. Dinkey No. 48 had red and green taillight markers as well as hooded dash floodlights under the front windows. It was built in 1902 by Kuhlman Car Company. (Courtesy of Mayor James W. Day.)

LAST DINKEY RIDE, APRIL 8, 1937. The dinkey was built in 1899, and its first run was in 1915. This picture shows the very last dinkey ride with William B. McDiarmid and Anthony W. Howe, who were the first passengers in 1915 as well as the last passengers on the last dinkey run. (Courtesy of Cuyahoga County Public Library Parma-South Branch.)

CHANGING OVER THE YEARS. The photograph above was taken in 1884 and shows the intersection of Pearl and York Roads, which is now located in Parma Heights. A tollbooth was originally placed in this area. The image below is from 1954 and shows the same location as above. Pearl Road used to be called Wooster Pike Road and was even referred to as the Three C Highway (Cleveland, Columbus, Cincinnati Highway). York Road was previously known as York Street and was called so because many settlers at that time arrived from New York. (Both courtesy of Parma Heights Historical Society.)

EARLY INTERSECTION. This image, taken in 1935, shows the intersection of Pearl and Snow Roads looking south on Pearl Road. Many of the early roads were named after the farmer who owned a major part of the nearby land. Other streets were sometimes named after the owner of the road itself. (Courtesy of Parma Area Historical Society.)

PEARL AND RIDGE, 1948. This intersection shows an aerial view of the site of the first settlers. Pearl and Ridge Roads intersect here, and at the time a variety of businesses were on all corners of the intersection. Even today this area continues to thrive. Parma Hardware and other older businesses are located here. (Courtesy of Parma Heights Historical Society.)

RAILWAY TRACKS. This c. 1915 photograph shows the Cleveland Railway Trackage along Wooster Pike (now Pearl Road). This was the early trolley line for the Cleveland Railway System and later became the bus-line route to Crile Hospital. This view is looking south toward the Ridge Road intersection. The Fay homestead was to the left of the mailboxes. (Courtesy of Parma Heights Historical Society.)

DENTZLER ROAD, 1946. The history of Dentzler Road goes back to 1852, as it was found on a map dating back to that time. H. and John Dentzer owned most of the land on Dentzler Road. The official dedication of this road was found to be on June 8, 1951. (Courtesy of Cleveland Press Collection.)

PARMA MUDDY STREETS, 1953. During the 1950s, there were about 90 unfinished streets in Parma. The streets had been dedicated but were never fully completed. In 1952, there were 85 miles of dirt roads and 75 miles of paved roads in the city. Eight years later, more streets became paved, and there were hardly any dirt roads left. Because of new laws, builders had to completely finish an area as part of their permission to build there. The photograph above shows Westminster Drive, while the image below is that of Belmere Drive. (Both courtesy of Cleveland Press Collection.)

PARMA HOUSING, 1973. On February 25, 1955, a significant zoning ordinance became a law. This ordinance regulated a more comprehensive zoning and districting of the city. Regulating the use of land, the city was divided into seven use districts: single-family house district, two-family house district, apartment-house district, retail-business district, commercial-manufacturing "A" district, commercial-manufacturing "B" district, and an industrial district. In this photograph, starting from the first diagonal street in the lower left-hand corner, are Gross Drive, Johnson Drive, Kader Drive, Bobko Boulevard, Ronald Drive, Schwab Drive, and Glamer Drive. This area is located in the southwestern part of the city. This image is a typical view of a residentially zoned area. All of these streets were named after developers, local families, or former mayors. (Courtesy of Cleveland Press Collection.)

RIDGEWOOD DRIVE, 1948. Previously known as Bean Road, it was changed to Ridgewood Drive as it extended from Parma to Seven Hills. Before roads were paved, they were dirt-filled roads, which made it easier for a horse and buggy to travel on. When cars were invented, they would often get stuck in the muddy dirt roads, which prompted the city to start paving them. (Courtesy of Cleveland Press Collection.)

LAKE OVERFLOW ON LONGWOOD AVENUE. This image from 1958 shows flooding caused from State Road Park (now Veterans Memorial Park) overflowing onto the streets. Many lakes and creeks were overloaded, causing basements to flood and streets to be covered with water. (Courtesy of Cleveland Press Collection.)

STREET NAME POLE, MAY 1962. Many gathered to watch street poles being painted at Ridge Road and Ridgewood Drive. They were painted aluminum so they would shine at night. Kneeling with the paint can is Edward Scalzitti, kneeling with the paintbrush is Len Schreiber, and standing on the stool is Mayor James W. Day. Ridgewood Drive was originally called Bean Road, named after the bean farmers in the area. Ridge Road was previously known as Center Road because it ran right through the center of the township. It was a red brick road and was said to be one of the nicest pavements in Ohio. Ridge Road is one of Parma's main roads as traffic arrives from Cleveland into Parmatown Mall as well as other residential sites. (Courtesy of Cleveland Press Collection.)

SNOW AND PEARL, 1956. This aerial view shows Snow Road (vertical road) at Pearl Road. The oval-shaped road is called Onaway Oval. Onaway Oval is part of Greenbriar Estates, which was an exclusive community in the 1940s through the 1960s. The top half of the photograph is Parma Heights, while the bottom half, separated by Snow Road, is Parma. (Courtesy of Mayor James W. Day.)

PARMA HOMES, 1959. In 1962, many numbered streets were changed to named streets. This picture shows West Ninety-eighth Street and West Ninety-sixth Street, which are now Whitaker Drive and Chateau Drive. To fill the population boom that happened in the 1960s, many developers came to the city to expand the residential area of Parma. (Courtesy of Cleveland Press Collection.)

PARMATOWN AREA, 1951. This aerial view shows the area of what is now Parmatown Mall and Ridge Road/Ridgewood Road. Pictured at the top left is Ridgewood Lake, and the vacant field to the top right is where Parmatown Mall now stands. The horizontal road at the bottom is Westminster Drive. In the 1960s, a proposed freeway would have taken out Westminster Drive and all the homes there, but the people opposed it and the freeway was never built. (Courtesy of Mayor James W. Day.)

BROADVIEW ROAD AREA. Shown here is Broadview Road intersecting with West Ridgewood Drive (top) and Grantwood (bottom). Broadview Road was first called Town Line Road, as it separated Parma Township from Independence Township. It was also a toll road at one time. Broadview Road became State Route 176 in 1947. (Courtesy of Mayor James W. Day.)

TRAFFIC JAM. This image from 1957 shows a traffic jam that resulted from a brush fire at West 130th Street and Brookpark Road. The view in this photograph is looking west. Brush fires are uncontrolled fires usually occurring where there are a lot of bushes and wilderness. (Courtesy of the Cleveland Press Collection.)

NEW DEVELOPMENTS. This image from 1959 shows the many homes that were springing up in the southern part of Parma. Crile Hospital is shown at the top, while a new development is being built between Pleasant Valley Road and West 121st Street, which is now known as Ann Arbor Drive. (Courtesy of Cleveland Press Collection.)

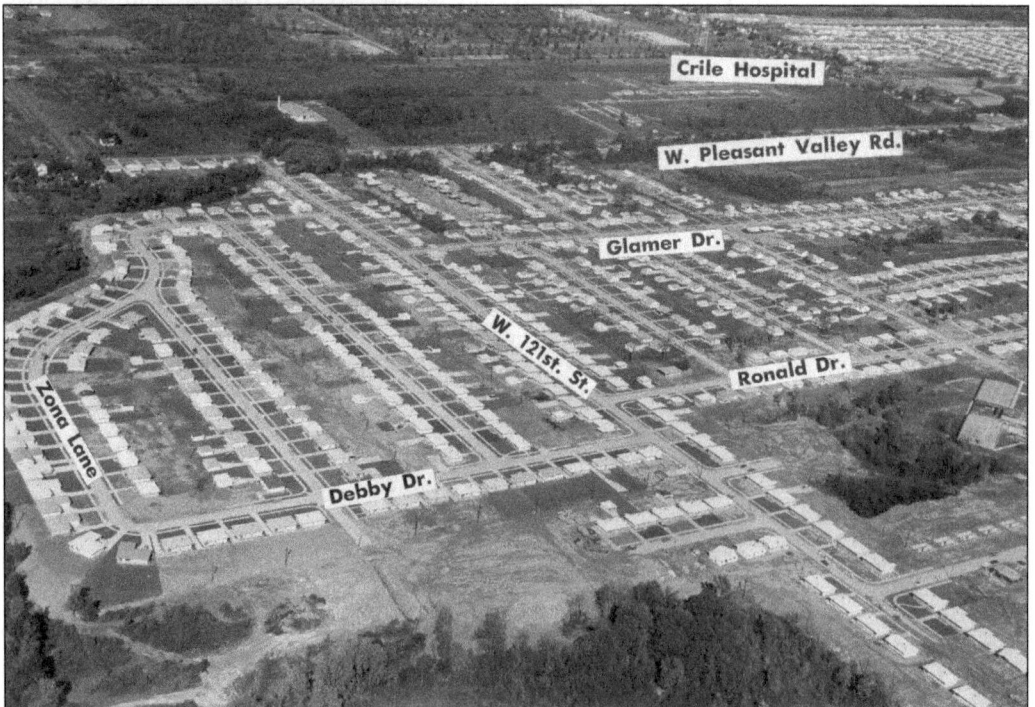

RUSH HOUR. This aerial view from 1959 shows a traffic jam at the Chevrolet plant at Brookpark and Stumph Roads. Traffic was often busy during rush hour around this time when there were many workers employed at the Chevrolet plant. (Courtesy of Cleveland Press Collection.)

RIDGE AND SOUTHINGTON. This image from 1951 shows the intersection of Ridge Road (horizontal) and Southington Drive. Ridgewood Golf Course is shown at the top, while a building located at the right of the photograph shows a Methodist church under construction. Southington Drive runs from West Fifty-fourth Street to Westminster Drive. (Courtesy of Mayor James W. Day.)

PARMA CIRCLE, 1971. The Parma Circle area was developed by Howard A. Stahl, who was a real estate developer in Parma in the 1920s. His goal for Parma Circle was to turn it into a community of upper-class residential homes. Stahl died in 1931 of heart failure at 56 years of age. (Courtesy of Cleveland Press Collection.)

PARMA HOUSING, 1970. Orchard Park Drive and Fruitland Drive were named so because they were developed in the middle of a large orchard. Holy Family Home can be seen in the upper left, as well as Statehouse Apartments in the lower right. (Courtesy of Cleveland Press Collection.)

Six

JUST PARMA

Parma is said to be named after a city in Italy. While it may share a similar name, its personality is far from the same. Many of the early settlers in Parma were of German descent. Over time, the city has become a mixture of different cultures. Parma's history is rich and has had many events for which it was made famous. In earlier times, Parma Day was a yearly celebration by the residents, as was the Ice Carnival, and later on Nationality Day made its way through the city to celebrate the diversity of its people. Other events, such as National Milk Week and Pancake Day, also helped to put Parma on the map.

While many people think that Parma may be just an average city, it has had some very interesting visitors. For instance, comedian Bob Hope made appearances in Parma. Other famous local personalities include Ghoulardi and Big Chuck. Actor and comedian Drew Carey had a theme song for his television show called "Moon Over Parma." More recently, he ordered 45 pizzas from his favorite pizza establishment, Antonio's Pizza in Parma, and had them delivered to him in California. Many political figures have also made appearances in the city. In 1980, Pres. Jimmy Carter came to Parma to speak with senior citizens and community leaders. Pres. Bill Clinton always made sure to make a stop at Parma Pierogies when campaigning in the city. In 2008, Hillary Clinton paid a visit to Grace's Grille on Pleasant Valley Road to talk about health care.

Parma may be a large community, but it still has that small-town feel that attracts a variety of people. Early settlers found the city attractive, and even today families that are looking for a close community find Parma an ideal city to live in. This chapter includes photographs that are uniquely related to Parma and its citizens.

PARMA CITY HALL, 1933. In 1924, Parma was incorporated as a village, and a new town hall was built. Previously, the former town hall had been in an old schoolhouse on Ridge and Bean Roads (Ridgewood Drive). This new hall was constructed on the east end of Ridge Road. (Courtesy of Cleveland Press Collection.)

CITY HALL. On January 1, 1931, Parma was declared a city. The first city council meeting occurred on January 5, 1931. During the time of the Depression in the 1930s, Parma was not growing, and there was talk of annexation to Cleveland, but instead a resolution was passed on January 15, 1931, to decrease the wage of every employee in Parma in order to recover some of the loss the city was experiencing. (Courtesy of Mayor James W. Day.)

EARLY RESIDENTS. Shown in this *c.* 1890 photograph are early members of St. Paulus Church. Around this time, the population of Parma Township grew in numbers as well as diversity. The 1870 census showed 1,500 people living in the township, mainly of German descent. (Courtesy of St. Paul United Church of Christ.)

REDRUP FAMILY. Shown here in 1916 is Tom Redrup shearing a sheep. His property was located at York and Sprague Roads. Members of the Redrup family were very early settlers in Parma. The Redrup house was built around 1850 and was a red brick house located at York and Sprague Roads. (Courtesy of the Kaiser family.)

PARMA RACES, AUGUST 1933. Many residents in Parma and surrounding cities celebrated Parma Day. This image shows one of the many races that took place, where people of all ages would compete for prizes. There was also a fat man's race, as well as a fat woman's race, where the winner would receive a case of beer. The big event of Parma Day, however, was the beauty contest in which the crowd chose the winner by clapping and whistling. (Courtesy of Cleveland Press Collection.)

PARMA DAY, 1940. As part of the Parma Day celebration, residents in this picture paraded in front of a movie camera in the center of town. The march was led by Mayor Roland Reichert and police chief Garry Burczyk. Parma Day was founded in 1919 and held yearly on the second Wednesday in August. (Courtesy of Cleveland Press Collection.)

PARMA ICE CARNIVAL. The Parma Ice Carnival was held in the 1930s. Skating championships were held and as many as 10,000 people would attend. Each pamphlet for the Ice Carnival was numbered, and the person holding the pamphlet with the winning number would win the grand prize. The image above shows the carnival being celebrated by residents, while the photograph to the right is an actual brochure from the event. The Ice Carnival was usually held at Ridgewood Lake, which was ideal for ice-skating in the winter months. (Above, courtesy of Cleveland Press Collection; at right, Cuyahoga County Public Library Parma-South Branch.)

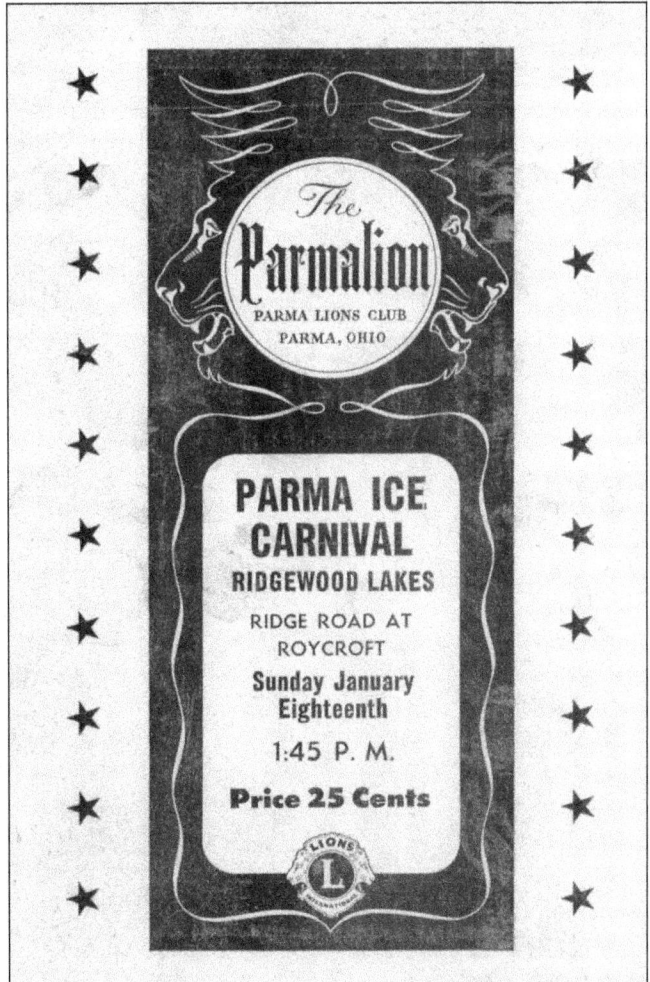

The
Parmalion
PARMA LIONS CLUB
PARMA, OHIO

PARMA ICE CARNIVAL
RIDGEWOOD LAKES
RIDGE ROAD AT ROYCROFT
Sunday January Eighteenth
1:45 P. M.
Price 25 Cents

GERMAN DAY, JUNE 16, 1940. After World War I, many Germans came to the United States and settled in Cleveland. In 1924, they established the German Central Organization. By 1926, the organization purchased land in Parma that became the German Central Farm and is used today as a recreation area for Cleveland's German population. (Courtesy of Cleveland Press Collection.)

GERMAN DAY, 1938. Big festivities are brewing during German Day at the German Central Farm. Band members, playing for a beer, performed at this event sponsored by the Federation of German Societies, which brought in over 3,000 people to the festival. (Courtesy of Cleveland Press Collection.)

RIDGEWOOD LAKE, 1968. Adults and children are enjoying a day of ice-skating at Ridgewood Lake. At the time, a red flag would go up on the flagpole telling the residents when the ice was unsafe to skate on. Ridgewood Lake used to be the site of the Uhinck family's farm, home of early settlers in Parma. (Courtesy of Cleveland Press Collection.)

FORESTWOOD RINK, 1964. Shown here are ladies enjoying their time at the Forestwood Ice Rink. It opened in 1959 as an outdoor rink and then became enclosed in 1983. The rink was officially dedicated in 1994 as the Michael A. Ries Ice Rink in honor of Michael Ries, who served as mayor from 1988 to 1994. (Courtesy of Cleveland Press Collection.)

ICE CARNIVAL, 1942. This image shows the victory march of Allied Nations at the Parma Ice Carnival. The United Nations was established in 1945 after World War II. (Courtesy of Cleveland Press Collection.)

STATE ROAD PARK, 1958. State Road Park, now called Veteran's Memorial Park, is a popular place for picnicking, baseball games, and walking. The National Softball Tournament was played there in 1966. The park has trails to walk on, as well as a lake to enjoy. (Courtesy of Cleveland Press Collection.)

114

HOERTZ FAMILY. This image, taken in 1911, shows the Hoertz family on their farm that was located on Hoertz Road across from St. Andrew Ukrainian Catholic Church. Some of the people in this photograph are standing on a Foos five-horsepower gas engine. A treadmill was located in the front of the barn in which the horses were attached. They would walk in a circle to grain livestock food. (Courtesy of Parma Area Historical Society.)

PARMA HOME. This home was located at Ridge and Pleasant Valley Roads. The photograph was taken in 1939, and the house at that time, which was situated on a 97-acre farm, was appraised for $14,850. (Courtesy of Cleveland Press Collection.)

WAGNER HOME. Shown here is the home of Bob Wagner on Ridge Road. The house is listed as a 1922 home in the county registry. There was previously an old barn on the property that was torn down, and part of the wood from this barn was used to build the garage that is there now. The house had a hand-pump water well and a potbellied stove. Wagner noted that Clevelanders used to refer to Parma as a "trip out to the country." (Courtesy of Bob Wagner.)

James Loder's Home. James Loder's farm was located on York Road but was later torn down to make way for a Peoples Savings and Loan bank. Loder and two other men were the last three trustees of Parma Township. They were responsible for turning over records and funds to Parma when it became a village. Shown here is the Loder family in 1931 at their farm on York and Pleasant Valley Roads. (Courtesy of the Kaiser family.)

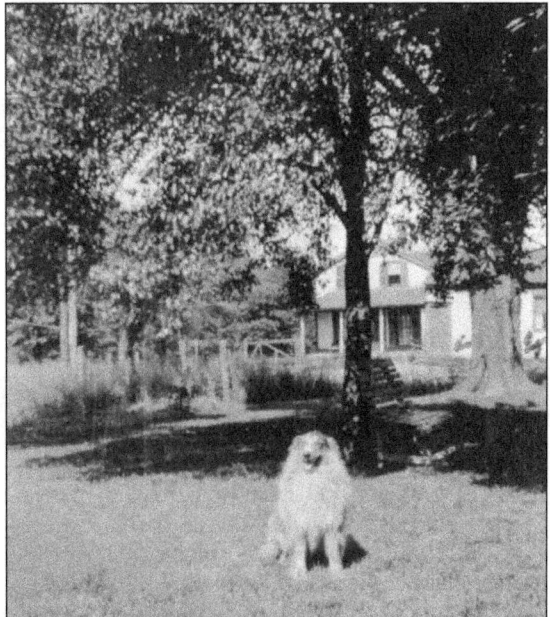

Early Building. The white building in the background was located at what is now the corner of York and Pleasant Valley Roads, where the Sunoco station now stands. Early church services were held here between 1852 and 1858 for members of St. Paulus Church. The building was later moved across the street and became a dance hall. (Courtesy of the Kaiser family.)

PARMA ROTARY CLUB AT STEARNS FARM. This photograph from 1981 shows members of the Parma Rotary Club taking a tour of Stearns Farm. The Parma Area Historical Society started in 1972 with a small group of residents interested in the history of the community. Volunteers have worked hard over the years to keep the farm running and restore the Gibbs house as well as the barn. (Courtesy of Cleveland Press Collection.)

HANRATTY'S BARN, DECEMBER 1957. This 90-year-old barn was owned by Edward J. Hanratty, a former Cuyahoga County sheriff. In 1957, the asking price for this 60-foot-high, 40-foot-by-80-foot-wide landmark was $1,700. Hanratty's barn was located on Gerald Avenue across from the old Parma police station. The barn was described as an early American political forum, as Democrats often met there for meetings. (Courtesy of Cleveland Press Collection.)

PANCAKE DAY. Mayor Joseph Kader stands here in 1958 with "Aunt Jemima." Kader declared September 28 to be "Pancake 'N Sausage Day." The Parma Junior Chamber of Commerce served all-you-can-eat pancakes and sausage on that day to everyone attending. The cost was 75¢ for children and $1.25 for adults. (Courtesy of Cleveland Press Collection.)

NATIONAL MILK WEEK, 1937. The National Milk Producers Federation and the Milk Industry Foundation started National Milk Week in 1937 in order to recognize the importance of the dairy industry to the nation's welfare. In the background are, from left to right, Margaret Gill Frey, C. F. Christian, C. J. Seegert; in the foreground is Mayor Roland Reichert. (Courtesy of Cuyahoga County Public Library Parma-South Branch.)

INTERIOR OF PARMA HOUSE, 1960. For the most part, the 1960s were a prosperous time all over the world, and many houses were built during this period. The home in this picture features an all-electric kitchen. Other amenities include copper tile, walnut-finished cabinets, a General Electric dishwasher, and a garbage disposer. (Courtesy of Cleveland Press Collection.)

BRIGGS BRANCH POST OFFICE, 1961. This post office, located on State Road, was named after Joseph Briggs. Around 1863, Briggs was a clerk in the Cleveland Post Office. During this time, there was no mail delivery, and many people would arrive at the post office and wait hours in line in order to send or receive mail. Briggs came up with a system of delivering mail to homes. (Courtesy of the Cleveland Press Collection.)

IRISH QUARTET. Shown here in 1928 is a Parmadale Irish quartet. This group sang tenor John McCormack's Irish songs for their performance. From left to right are James Dolan, Raymond McGorray, Peter McDermott, and Kenneth Rhodey. Boys at Parmadale would rehearse every day for the big Christmas show put on every year. (Courtesy of Cleveland Press Collection.)

NATIONALITY DAY, 1977. Nationality Days were an annual celebration full of ethnic food and dances. Parma would show its appreciation of the varied groups in the community by having this celebration. It was held in Parmatown Mall and had dancing, singing, art, and food from over 25 ethnic groups. Some of the many groups represented were Arabic, Bavarian, British, Chinese, Egyptian, German, Greek, Hawaiian, Italian, Jewish, Polish, Ukrainian, Romanian, Serbian, and Turkish. (Courtesy of Cleveland Press Collection.)

MEMORIAL DAY, 1979. Shown here are flags flying in front of the Parma Municipal Auditorium for a Memorial Day celebration. Parma's first annual Memorial Day was celebrated in 1868 and continues to this day at the Parma Heights Cemetery along Pearl Road. (Courtesy of Cleveland Press Collection.)

PARMADALE BAND. Parmadale bands became very popular in the city and performed at many parades and concerts. They often played at the Parma Day festivals each year. They also marched at the St. Patrick's Day Parade in Cleveland. Under the direction of Jack Hearns, the band would dress in full uniform to give its performance. As well as playing instruments, children at Parmadale also sang, acted in plays, learned popular dances such as the waltz and fox trot, and participated in other cultural events. (Both courtesy of Cleveland Press Collection.)

PARMADALE FOOTBALL. Dominic Fontana is shown on September 1, 1937, carrying the ball for Parmadale in a game that ended with a score of 0-0. Parmadale had many athletic teams in various sports such as softball, horseshoes, volleyball, track, and football. (Courtesy of Cleveland Press Collection.)

PARMA BAND. This is the Parma High School Marching Band in 1978. The band was featured in a parade scene in the 1983 movie *A Christmas Story.* The band director at the time was Jim Sentz. (Courtesy of Cleveland Press Collection.)

GHOULARDI, 1964. Ghoulardi was a character created by disc jockey Ernie Anderson. From 1963 to 1966, he was the late night host of *Shock Theater*. Ghoulardi's ethnic humor included jokes about Parma, which he commonly called "Amrap" (Parma spelled backwards). His unmerciful jokes on Parma's working-class, "white sock"–wearing residents ultimately led to a series of skits called Parma Place. Ghoulardi (center) is pictured here with John Bellas (left) and Mayor James W. Day. (Courtesy of Cleveland Press Collection.)

BIG CHUCK AND LITTLE JOHN, 1979. Chuck Schodowski (right) and John Rinaldi (left) became a big part of the community. Linked to the Ghoulardi era, Schodowski helped to put "a certain ethnic group" on the map. He was later joined by Bob "Hoolihan" Wells, who was later replaced by "Lil' John" Rinaldi to form the *Big Chuck and Lil' John* show. In 2009, Mayor Dean DePiero presented Schodowski with a key to the city of Parma. (Courtesy of Cleveland Press Collection.)

PARMADALE BOYS. Parmadale has been a steady fixture in Parma for over 80 years. When Parmadale opened its doors, it was the largest group of buildings in the nation related to a Catholic charity. This 1940s-image shows the boys of Parmadale Children's Village raising the American flag to show their patriotism. Parmadale was a home for troubled children that was started in 1925. (Courtesy of Cuyahoga County Library Parma-South Branch.)

BIBLIOGRAPHY

Day, James W. *Parma Day*. Ohio: George Cormack, 2005.

Horley, Robert. *The Best Kept Secrets of Parma, "The Garden City"*. Ohio: self-published, 1998.

Kubasek, Ernest. *The History of Parma*. Ohio: Ernest Kubasek and Bernard Survoy, 1976.

The Parma Historic Keepsake Committee. *Parma Sesquicentennial 1826–1976*. Ohio: The Parma Historic Keepsake Committee, 1976.

Turner, James. *The Heritage of Parma Heights*. Ohio: The Heritage of Parma Heights Committee, 1969.

Visit us at
arcadiapublishing.com

www.ingramcontent.com/pod-product-compliance
Lightning Source LLC
Chambersburg PA
CBHW050713110426
42813CB00007B/2174